COUTURE CROCHET workshop

COUTURE CROCHET workshop

Mastering Fit, Fashion, and Finesse

Lily M. Chin

DEDICATION

This is for everyone who's helped to make me the crocheter that I am today. To Mom, of course, who gave me the basics of crochet at an early age (I believe I was eight). There was also cousin Esther and my "cum-moh," or auntie on my mother's side. This was part of the extended family that helped to pass the craft down to yet another generation. Mrs. Collette must be mentioned. My fifth-grade teacher actually started an after-school crochet club! Jill Kellner, Joanne Civitano, Rita Silver, Sheila Hicks, Debra and Nancy Chin—they were all there, an encouraging entourage. Sandy's mother, Ms. Babad (my music teacher), and the security guards further helped me along by purchasing crocheted items from me in junior high school.

Thanks to all in the garment industry for edifying my skills, despite forced labor practices (grin). Everyone from Julio and Carlos in the sample room to Carolina Amato (who had me manufacturing to pay my way through college) to Nancy Winarick (whose connections got me jobs with the "big names") must be mentioned.

To the early editors, Annemarie Lawson of the now-defunct *McCall's Needlework and Crafts*, Janice Utter of early *Crochet Fantasy*, Kathleen Neville of *Fashion Crochet*, and Barbara Rondeau from *Leisure Arts*. They believed in me.

Then there are the others who in some way have touched my crochet life: all the crocheters I've crossed paths with, students who've taken my classes, colleagues like Arlene Mintzer, Peggy Grieg, Michelle Maks-Thompson, and Jacqui Henderson. They've inspired and contributed in infinite and countless ways.

Text © 2006, Lily M. Chin
Illustration © 2006, Interweave Press LLC
Photography © 2006, Interweave Press LLC unless otherwise noted.
Photography © 2006, Jayne Wexler, pages: 5, 10, 11, 12, 20, 21, 24, 26, 32, 38

INTERWEAVE PRESS

Interweave Press LLC
201 East Fourth Street
Loveland, CO 80537-5655 USA
www.interweave.com

Printed and bound in China through Pimlico.

Library of Congress Cataloging-in-Publication Data

Chin, Lily M.
  Couture crochet workshop : mastering fit, fashion, and finesse / Lily M. Chin.
     p. cm.
  Includes bibliographical references and index.
  ISBN 10:1-59668-008-3 (pbk.)
       13: 978-1-59668-008-1(pbk.)
  1. Crocheting—Patterns. I. Title.
  TT825.C392 2006
  746.43'40432—dc22

                                  2006012379

10 9 8 7 6 5 4 3 2 1

Acknowledgments

As the saying goes, no man is an island and no author does it alone. Thanks to Betsy Armstrong, Linda Stark, and Linda Ligon, who coerced me into doing yet another book with Interweave (no arm-twisting tactics were employed!). Of course, editors Karen Manthey and Jennifer Worick saved my skin, and JC Briar came through at the last minute. Annie Bakken, Rebecca Campbell, and Paulette Livers treated me with infinite patience and never once yelled at me when I was bad. Mel Young and Amy Chin were always there for me, loaning out spaces and playing gopher and porter. Can you imagine how lucky I felt employing the photographic services of portrait artist extraordinaire Jayne Wexler?

Naturally, gratitude is expressed to those yarn companies and suppliers for providing our materials, especially Eric and Paul Nichols. I must not forget dear pal and consultant, Barbara Hillery, founder and past president of the New York City Crochet Guild. Then there are the tireless stitchers—Joann Moss yet again comes through for me, as does Marge Scensny.

Lastly, most love and appreciation goes to my husband and best friend, Clifford Pearson. Once more, he played the role of a craft book widower!

Contents

Welcome to the Couture Crochet Workshop

Crochet has long suffered a dowdy reputation. Images of toilet paper rolls and tissue box covers come to mind at the mere mention of the word. Miles of afghans, though comforting on cold nights, usually translate into lots of bulk with little drape. Thus, the common conception is that crocheted items are stiff and boxy. That's all changed.

With the recent resurgence of crocheted fashions, lace in particular, crochet has shed its old-fashioned image. And I'm glad to be part of this upswing, as my crocheted creations for the collections of Isaac Mizrahi, Vera Wang, Diane von Furstenberg, and Ralph Lauren have graced the runways or catwalks of New York City's fashion week since the mid-1990s.

But what exactly is "couture?" Technically speaking, true *haute couture* is a protected term in France. There are rules, according to the Chambre Syndicale de la Couture Parisienne, the official regulating commission that oversees the qualifications (it even has its own school!). According to Chambre Syndicale de la Couture Parisienne rules, to classify as a couture house, a couturier must produce fifty new, original designs of day and evening wear for each collection. They must show two collections a year. They must employ a minimum of at least twenty full-time technical people in at least one atelier or workshop.

Because of the strict regulations by the Chambre, only a few design houses can use the exclusive "Haute Couture" label. Currently, there are only nine high-ranking couture houses, including Chanel, Christian Dior, Givenchy, Jean Paul Gaultier, Christian Lacroix, and American Ralph Rucci and his Chado label. The current couture classification houses are entitled to free advertising on state-run French television.

Couturelike Quality

Here in the United States, while there is no "true" couture, we can come very close. True couture specifically means that a garment or outfit is fitted exactly to each and every client. Hence, price tags can soar into the five- and sometimes six-figure range. It's not out of the question to find ball gowns priced at $25,000 to $30,000. Only socialites, royalty, celebrities, and lottery winners can afford most haute couture. I'm irked that Americans repeatedly misuse the phrase and bandy it about liberally. I've worked for many high-end designers and none of their lines or labels, even the most expensive, can truly be defined as true haute couture. They are all ready-to-wear, despite their exceptional quality.

But couture*like* quality can be had. Here's how:

- **Customizations.** If we fit to perfection and cater to a very specific body, we follow the tradition of couture.

Above: Lily loves to fondle yarns of every fiber, color, and texture.

Opposite: Lily consults with assistant, Mel, on a fashion sketch.

blend such as wool/polyester/acrylic, and mid-level lines, sometimes known as "career" or "bridge," may use pure wool.

- **Fashion.** Lastly, there is a certain sense of fashion that elevates a garment. Born and raised in New York City, I live and breathe fashion. Any crocheter, however, can take inspiration from fashion magazines and catalogs. Look online, on television, or in print for coverage of the runway shows that make up "fashion week" (which happens twice a year). Frequent malls and boutiques to find design ideas.

The Couture Crochet Workshop

It is my goal to empower you with the knowledge and ability to adapt and even design from scratch your own ideas, and to fit your garments well. I hope the designs in this book can function as a jumping-off point or inspiration for your own ideas and designs. Sometimes, you might find it necessary to design your own crocheted garment. For instance, how often do you find yourself frustrated because you can't find patterns in the perfect size? Or if you do find one, it fits everything but the shoulders or hips or arms? Customizing designs allows you to customize fit, and with this book, you'll gain the tools so you can make adjustments to your garments and guarantee a superb fit.

While I also present smaller projects in the form of accessories, the focus is on garments. Crocheted fashions, specifically well-made and fine-fitting ones, are sorely lacking in the market. Here, I've put together a collection of stylish and elegant wearables. But I don't ignore accessories, because they can make a more complete, cohesive, *finished* look. Besides, they can be quick and fun to make. But above all, I wish to impart the ability to create your own customized clothing. Join me in this venture and you'll find yourself "hooked," so to speak.

- **Fine finishing.** If you can focus on making the inside of your look every bit as good as the outside, you're that much closer to achieving a couture look.
- **Details.** Don't forget the details that come with hand finishing. With crochet, there is no such thing as a crocheting machine (well, other than me!). Thus, any crocheted piece is by nature and default handmade. This type of intensive labor also garners higher prices. In general, the more details, the higher the cost. That extra collar, pocket, or lining means more time and care.
- **Fabrication.** Luxe materials add a couturelike quality. The upper "signature" collections use cashmere, whereas lower-priced lines may use a fiber

ONE

Laying the Foundation

Let me provide some insight into the finer points of stitching crochet. I am going to assume that the reader has the basic foundation and knowledge to create all standard stitches. If you need assistance or a refresher course, there are many good books on crochet basics.

The Turning Chain

Even if one is an advanced beginner, a confusing aspect when working back and forth is the use of the turning chain. Whereas a chain-2 replaces the first stitch in half-double crochet, a chain-3 replaces the first stitch in double-crochet, and a chain-4 replaces the first stitch in treble-crochet at the beginning of rows, the use of the chain-1 in single crochet does not substitute for the first stitch. That is, after chaining 1, a single crochet is indeed worked into the first stitch at the beginning of the row.

That being said, I truly despise that extra space at the beginning of half-double crochet and double-crochet rows (right).

To avoid this space at the beginning of half-double crochet and double-crochet rows, I suggest using what I call a "loosened, elongated chain" that does *not* count as a stitch (just as in single crochet). To work this, loosen up the loop that's on the hook slightly, work a loose chain, and again slightly loosen up the loop that's on the hook (see page 15, top right).

What this loosened, elongated chain does is get the work to the proper height of the stitch(es) to be worked on that particular row. Since it does not substitute or take the place of the first stitch, and the first stitch is indeed being worked into, there is no space.

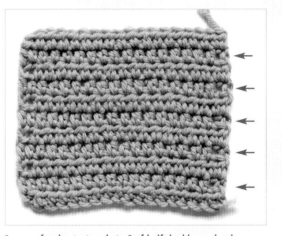

Spaces after beginning chain-2 of half-double crochet leave gaps

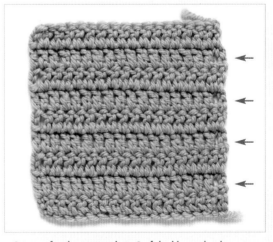

Spaces after beginning chain-3 of double crochet leave gaps

13

Loosened chain at beginning of half-double crochet rows eliminates gaps

Loosened chain at beginning of double crochet rows eliminates gaps

While there is a bit more "stuff" at the side edges of every alternate row, it is minimal since this loosened chain, when stretched, becomes much narrower than the chain-3 that is usually used. Furthermore, when seaming or applying a trim, it is a big plus not to have gaping spaces. The best part is that there is no working into the top of a chain-3 at the end of the rows—just leave the loosened chain-1 alone and do not work into it at all.

Note: While I prefer this elongated chain at the beginning of rows, the directions in this book are written in the "standard" manner. Substitute these beginning chains if you wish.

The Foundation Chain

Just about all of crochet begins with the foundation chain. Yet this chain is invariably too tight. This is the bane and scourge of crocheters.

To alleviate this, I suggest using a hook one or two sizes larger than called for in the pattern, just for the chain. Just don't forget to change back to the original size after working the chain.

If the chain is still too tight, or if the gauge is so loose that it becomes too difficult to work into, consider using a double strand of yarn just for the foundation chain.

Mary Rhodes of California, however, deserves accolades for coming up with a method of creating the chain *at the same time* you work the stitch. This is for a solid row of stitches, not lace. View this technique at http://hometown.aol.com/Sbaycgoa/foundatn.htm.

The big advantage of this method, besides a looser foundation chain, is that you never run out of chains, nor are there any leftover extra chains if you don't happen to chain the right number from the start. This method is also great when having to add several stitches at the end of a row (chain at the beginning to gain several stitches).

When going into the foundation chain, I often prefer not to go under the usual top two strands of the chain. Instead, I like to rotate the chain around until you see the back bump of the chain (it looks like a purl stitch in knitting). See illustration at opposite page top left.

By going into this single back bump, the full chain will remain in full view at the bottom and will match the top edge.

Binding Off

When having to lop off several stitches at once at the beginning of a row (such as when shaping for the armhole or sloped shoulders), the traditional convention is to slip-stitch across those unwanted stitches. Instead of slip-stitching across these stitches, which renders the

Working into the back bump of foundation chain

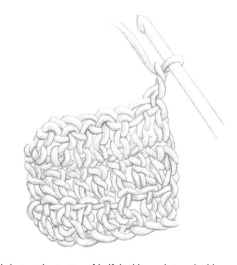
Elongated chain at beginning of half-double crochet or double crochet rows

fabric much bulkier, I end off the work at the beginning of the row by drawing the ball of yarn through the last loop (right, middle).

To begin again, leave a loose strand of yarn over the stitches that would normally have slip stitches over them and draw yarn through the first stitch to be worked, then chain for the beginning of the row (right, bottom).

Later on, this loose strand may be caught while seaming or trimming. *Note:* While I prefer this method over slip-stitching at the beginning of rows, the directions in this book are written in the "standard" manner. Substitute those beginning slip stitches if you wish to do so.

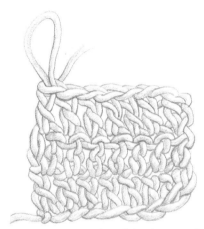
Drawing yarn through last loop to end off

Seaming

Mattress seam is my seam of choice, as I find it the least bulky. It is also easier to work as the right side, or public side, of the pieces face you at all times. This is a standard technique and can be found in any good "how to crochet" book.

I've tried to keep seams to a minimum in this book. If not worked seamlessly in the round (via the use of the slip stitch to join last stitches to first stitches), pieces are often worked all at the same time. The cardigan sweaters, for instance, have Back, Left Front, and Right Front pieces all worked as one. Sleeves, however, due to the more involved shaping of the cap, usually have to be set in. But hey, at least they are small.

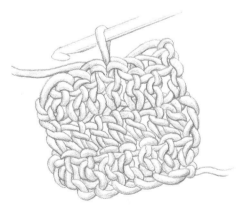
Starting strand of yarn a few stitches inwards

Swatch

Treat the swatch as you would the ultimate project. Do you ever intend on laundering the garment? Well, wash the swatch! Figure out ahead of time if the colors will run or if the dimensions will shrink or grow. Put it in a pocket for a few days to see if the yarn will hold up to wear and tear. Will it pill? Do unto the swatch what you will do unto the project. In this way, you can "predict the future" and avoid any surprises.

I know this does not seem spontaneous. We all chomp at the bit, itching to get to the project immediately. A little planning and foresight, however, will save a lot of heartache in the long run. I'd rather spend half an hour and half a skein of yarn and do this kind of testing, than spend four months and fourteen balls of yarn only to be disappointed when all is said and done.

For those who are confirmed nonswatchers and steadfastly refuse to do the swatch, all I can say is . . . you reap what you sow, or in this case, crochet.

Blocking

I can't emphasize this enough: blocking is one of those overlooked tools that can take a project from looking homemade to handcrafted. In the garment industry, the finisher has the most highly paid position at a factory. This final phase in mass production can make or break the whole line. When things are shipped to the stores, garments must look professional and flawless or they run the risk of being returned.

The finisher uses serious steam presses, the kind that have a clamper part that comes down over the fabric and releases sauna bursts that could seriously clean out your pores. It is this final action that removes any irregularities in the garment, but more importantly, determines the final measurements and therefore the size of a piece. It's the element of *heat* that renders the fabric nearly immutable.

Though you may not necessarily want a commercial look to your sweaters, if you want to block garments

A steamed and flat vs an unsteamed and curling swatch

more permanently to a given size, I strongly suggest not just wet-blocking, but adding heat as well, via steam.

It all begins with the *swatch*. You find out from your swatch what the ultimate steamed, stretched, and maxed-out gauge is, and you can use this to match the pattern. Thus, the before-gauge is no doubt smaller than the after-gauge.

Steam blocking relaxes the gauge. After steaming, wool might lose a bit of spring and loft as it softens. Steaming can add more slink to a rayon or silk. I often crochet slightly tighter than normal, and then make sure I hit the gauge after steam blocking.

I am a confirmed steamer and have converted many others when I convinced them to try it. I steam just about everything, including acrylic, because it "sets" the stitches in place better than just wetting it down and drying (think about what hot rollers can do for hair), and at the same time relaxes and evens out the stitches. I've even steamed metallics! It alleviated the slight scratchiness on the *Sports Illustrated* crocheted string bikini that I created several years ago.

The most important things to remember: use a terrific steam iron *without ever* touching the hot iron to fabrics and allow the piece to dry thoroughly. I have a professional steamer used by dry cleaners that looks like a vacuum cleaner hose hooked up to a water cooler. It produces enough steam to remove ancient wallpaper! It's also great for facials (just kidding).

I have several blocking anecdotes, but my favorite is how I salvaged a dear friend's cotton chenille tunic. She had worked it in the round and it was six inches too narrow. On the verge of tears, she was skeptical when I offered to "grow" it for her. Figuring she had nothing to lose, she let me work my magic. I proceeded to run blocking wires up the sides and stretch the dickens out of it until it was the desired width. I then proceeded to steam both sides until it was saturated—almost drenched—in moisture. When the piece dried, not only did it stay the proper size, but the stitches appeared more even and the cotton chenille was softened, thus enhancing wearability.

An added bonus is that the curl that is endemic to a lot of crochet can be blocked out, especially with steam. Don't take just my word for it. Do some testing on your own. Make two swatches of the same yarn. Steam one and set it next to the nonsteamed swatch, and compare. Or you can try steaming part of one swatch and comparing it to the other untouched half.

Killing a Fabric

There is an industry term: "killing a fabric." To do this, very carefully press the fabric with a hot iron. This permanently changes the look, feel, drape, body, and texture. Whether this is a good or bad thing is totally up to the project and the individual. Many like a "dressier" sheen and lustrous drape. An added bonus is that once "killed," the stitches are set for life (a bit of a oxymoron, I know). It will grow no longer, shrink no further, and remain relatively immutable. Again, it is the gauge after killing that should match the pattern's gauge. This, too, can be done on synthetics, provided a pressing cloth is put over the project, unless you *like* sticky irons.

Some people like spring and loft in a fabric, as in a baby afghan, for example. If this is the desired effect, do not kill your work, just wet block a little. For other items, such as a skirt or tank top, where more drape is desirable, by all means, maim if not totally kill your garment. Especially on larger pieces, killing stabilizes the fabric so that it will not morph into a lumpy potato sack.

Let the project determine whether killing is appropriate or not. Most certainly do it on the swatch first, especially when killing can radically alter your stitch gauge (but not your criminal record). Trying it out on a swatch is even more important considering that, as in real life, once killed, there's no hope of resuscitation.

Killing can lead to many garment possibilities not traditionally thought of in crocheting, such as slinky lingerie or evening wear (slips, camisoles, nighties). It can add swing to a skirt, hang to a hem, sharpness to a shawl. . . . You get the idea.

I've not killed often, I confess—I tend more toward maiming with steam—but when I have had to, I was glad I did. I created a lace evening dress in rayon for designer Isaac Mizrahi's label. The yarn kinked up while I crocheted it and the lace had no definition. Once I pressed it open, the yarn behaved and the pattern was flawlessly evident. The sheen made the gown glow and the fabric was sinuous.

Hung Gauge

Do you wear your crocheted garments only while lying in bed? No? Then why determine gauge from a swatch laying flat on a table? Instead, hang it vertically—the way the garment is to be worn. Use push-pins on a cork board, straight pins on a towel hanging on a rack, or even masking tape. If the yarn is particularly dense (cotton, silk, linen, rayon), apply a few clothespins along the bottom since the larger piece as a whole will be weighty (below).

Emulate real life as much as possible. This will be the true gauge when worn, and the gauge you should use when matching a pattern or creating a design. If a piece elongates (and how often have we had sweaters in a nonresilient yarn like cotton grow on us?), it also usually narrows in width. There's only so much yarn in there. If it gives one way, it will take from somewhere else.

After-gauge

In conclusion, when directions say "block the piece to measurements," what I mean is block to achieve the ultimate "after-gauge," the one that matches the directions postwashing, blocking, and hanging. Furthermore, I always believe smaller is better since you can always stretch and block. It's much more difficult to shrink a garment.

Hanging swatch with clothespin weights

TWO

Reading Charts

The Japanese are pioneers of the international system of charting patterns. They found that by using symbols for stitches rather than writing out everything fully, not only do you save on a lot of space and repetition, you can transcend language so that any culture can understand the patterns. An added bonus is that symbols are great "visualizing" tools. You can see what has to be done at a glance, where the piece is going, and where it has been. This is a boon to figuring out shapes.

The standard symbols are illustrated here:

STITCH KEY

⬯ = chain (ch)

+ = single crochet (sc)

T = double crochet (dc)

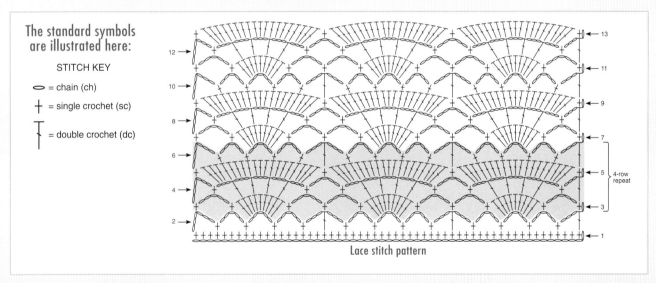

Lace stitch pattern

The above reads as:

Ch 60.

Row 1 (RS): Sc in 2nd ch from hook and in each ch across—59 sc.

Row 2 (WS): Ch 6 and turn (counts as a dc and ch-3), skip first 3 sc, *sc in next sc, [ch 5, skip next 3 sc, sc in next sc] 3 times, ch 3, skip 2 sc, dc in next sc **, ch 3, skip 2 sc; rep from * across, end last rep at **.

Row 3: Ch 1 and turn, sc in first dc, *ch 5, sc in next ch-5 lp, 9 dc in next ch-5 lp, sc in next ch-5 lp, ch 5, sc in next dc; rep from * across, end last sc in 3rd ch of

beg ch-6 instead of into a dc.

Row 4: Ch 6 and turn (counts as a dc and ch-3), *sc in next ch-5 lp, [ch 3, skip next dc, dc in next dc] 4 times, ch 3, sc in next ch-5 lp **, ch 5; rep from * across, end last rep at **, ch 3, dc in last sc.

Row 5: Ch 1 and turn, sc in first dc, skip 3 ch and next sc, *[3 dc in next ch-3 lp, dc in next dc] 4 times, 3 dc in next ch-3 lp, sc in next ch-5 lp; rep from * across, end last sc in 3rd ch of beg ch-6 instead of into ch-5 lp.

Row 6: Ch 6 and turn (counts as a dc and ch-3), *[skip 3 dc, sc in next dc, ch 5] 3 times, skip 3 dc, sc in next

19

dc, ch 3, dc in next sc **, ch 3; rep from * across, end last rep at **.

Rep Rows 3 through 6 for pattern.

Notice how Right Side rows are read from right to left, and Wrong Side rows are read from left to right? Also note that although you turn your work, the chart only represents the one side—the Right Side—at all times.

By seeing how patterned stitches are constructed, irregular shapes such as necklines and waist shaping can be mapped out. How often have you started a project using a fancier stitch pattern, only to get stuck when it's time to shape the armhole? Having a stitch chart will allow you to find ways around this. You will be able to "scratch out" parts of the pattern that need to be taken away. Sounds like fun, doesn't it? Don't worry; we'll discuss this further in later chapters.

THREE

Planning Your Own Patterns

When I was thirteen, I worked in the sweatshops of New York's Chinatown during the summer and, sometimes, after school. My mother was the forelady at a factory and my older sister was the bookkeeper. I did all kinds of odd jobs, including the payroll. If the buttonholer was out sick, I did buttonholing. If the thread cutter couldn't make it, I cut thread. It was here that I learned garment making from the ground up.

I apprenticed with Julio and Carlos, the flat-pattern drafters. I was surrounded by patterns on heavy card stock. Even though I was a miserable seamstress who could barely sew a straight seam, I knew the concepts and theories of fitting.

As a crocheter, I had no notion of gauge; I didn't know what the word meant. I instinctively knew, however, that if a flat pattern fit me, all I had to do was make sure that my crocheting followed the same shapes as that pattern, and the finished garment would ultimately fit me.

Thus, I would frequently hold my work up to that flat sewing pattern to make sure I was on track. I'd see that the work had to narrow on the sides, then widen out again. I'd check it every couple of rows. I still do this on occasion. When given a flat pattern (as often happens when working with retail designers), I even use that flat pattern as my template for blocking.

Getting Basic Patterns and Measurements

Flat Sewing Patterns

So you have in mind some kind of garment that you want to make. Is it a jacket? A skirt? How do you come up with the pattern and measurements? There are a few options. Like me, you can start with a sewing pattern as your base. Just make sure the pattern actually fits you. How, exactly? In sewing, a mock-up or dummy, often referred to as a "muslin," is used. It is called a muslin because that's the fabric used for the mock-up.

Alas, our crocheted fabrics bear very little resemblance to muslin; unlike crochet, muslin has no stretch and is quite thin and filmy. Instead, use inexpensive polar fleece or sweatshirt fabric, or even stretch-knit sweater yardage. These all have the same heft and stretch as crocheting. Choose a fabric that's as close to the real thing as possible.

Use sewing patterns meant for stretch fabric as well. They will have less fussy shaping details. Some things that are included in a woven pattern, such as elbow darts, are wholly unnecessary in stretch fabric. Other simplifications may be employed. Instead of asymmetrical sleeve caps and different front and back armholes, keep it simple. Use the same shaping for both armholes and make the sleeve cap symmetrical.

Construct this sample mock-up with these stretchy, heavier fabrics and refine the fit on the body. Where it is too tight, loosen it. Where it is too long, shorten it. Once you're happy with your "muslin," carefully mark all the seams, and then take it apart. Your crocheting can follow this newly fitted pattern and will fit in the same way. Make sure you eliminate the seam allowances.

Another nice outcome of this process is that if you reassemble the muslin, you'll have another garment to boot!

Draping

Another approach is to drape a pattern directly on the body. This is a more advanced approach, one that took me at least two courses at New York City's Fashion Institute of Technology to master. To do this, use the same types of fabrics mentioned before: polar fleece, sweatshirt fabric, or stretch-knit sweater yardage. The bonus from the first two is that the cut edges will not fray. It's even better if you can find these fabrics with a plaid or grid pattern, ensuring that the lines stay straight, or "plumb."

Using the fabric, "build" the sweater right onto the body. Doing this on yourself can be awkward and inaccurate, so use a dress dummy or form. One can make a very good "double" with kits (available from sewing sources) that employ duct tape and Styrofoam. If not, find a skilled, reliable buddy who is good with his or her hands (having a garment-making background obviously helps), and who won't use you as a life-size voodoo doll and stick you with pins.

Once you've put together a garment that fits, mark seams carefully, take it apart, and follow the same steps as the muslin from a flat sewing pattern. I give references for further investigation in the Sources and Further Reading section in the back of the book (see page 159).

Existing Patterns

If these pattern-making techniques seem daunting to you, and the silhouette of your intended garment is rather simple, make use of existing crochet patterns. If you have your heart set on a V-necked pullover with set-in sleeves, find one in the many magazines and books and leaflets that are on the market already.

Again, check for the fit. Have you made this before? Did it fit you? If not, how can you modify it so that it does? If you have something that worked before, or if you know what adjustments are needed, use this as the basis or template from which to create new patterns.

Even if you never plan to make any of the patterns from a book or a magazine, I suggest studying the schematic measurements. It's useful to see what are considered "standard" measurements, and then tweak them to your liking. For instance, how wide is an average crewneck opening? How deep is it in front? How deep is a standard armhole for a drop-shouldered sleeve? These are good things to note.

Existing Garments

Look to your closet! Take out all the clothes that fit. They don't have to be crocheted. Try them on. Note how they fit (loose, snug, over-sized, etc.). Then take a tape measure to them and jot down the dimensions. While you're at it, write down what kind of fabric (stretchy, thin, etc.) each garment is made of.

In the garment industry, there is such a thing as making a "rub-off," using the actual garment to create a paper pattern. I start with a large pad of gridded "flip chart" paper from an office supply store. This is much easier to find and the grids are easier to see than the blue dots on industry "marker paper." The large sheet size also ensures that I can get whole garment pieces onto one sheet. The lines of the grid are usually 1 inch apart, which is very convenient.

I then fold the garment in half and line it up against the side edge of the paper that I've marked as the "fold line" or "center line." Everything from here is just a mirror image. Trace the outlines of the garment onto the gridded paper. To navigate around curves such as an armhole, use a straight pin to puncture holes onto the paper and make markings. Later, with the aid of a French curve and pencil, smooth out a curve over these puncture holes. Voilà: a rubbed-off paper pattern from your existing clothes.

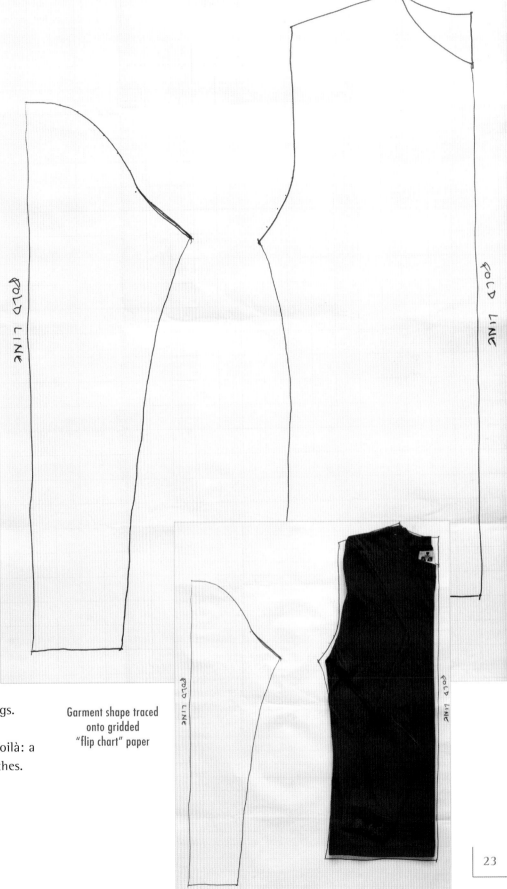

Garment shape traced
onto gridded
"flip chart" paper

B1

A2

B2

C2

Computer Software

There are a few programs on the market specifically made for knitting, and crocheters can use them as well. These work only if you're crocheting a solid fabric of basic stitches and the stitches are stacked on top of one another in a gridlike formation (like most knitting stitches). You plug in the gauge, choose your size, shapes, styles, and dimension, and the program spits out patterns for you to follow.

There are also computer programs, some made for sewing, that will generate life-sized paper patterns for you to use as a template. Many sheets of standard paper must be taped together to achieve the full pattern. I personally like and use Garment Designer from Cochenille, since it can generate both knitting and sewing patterns. Use whatever helps you achieve your dream garment!

Above: Lily creates a pattern on grid paper
Left and opposite: Garment pattern generated from computer software

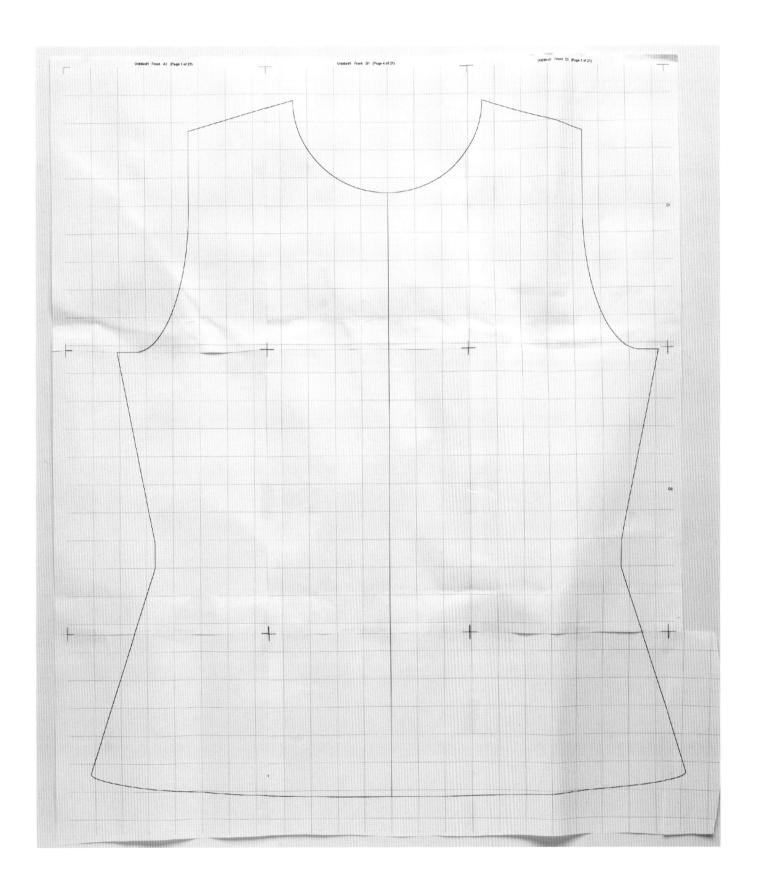

FOUR

Refinements in Fitting

I've already mentioned the importance of fit when creating a couturelike garment. Every body has different considerations—long torso, ample bust, short arms—and while most patterns provide a guideline to creating a garment that will more or less fit, this chapter will give you tools to modify an existing pattern or design your own pattern for a perfect fit.

Ease

As I wrote earlier, garments can fit us in many ways from spray-painted-on tight to circus-tent huge. Women's clothing offers greater range than men's garments. Fashion and preference play a big role as well. In the 1980s, baggy and oversized was all the rage. Recently, close-fitting clothing has become more the norm.

In crochet, one can actually have a garment measure less than you do, since the fabric will stretch somewhat. This is not the case with nonstretch woven items. Generally speaking, most of the garments we make will have a bit of "room" between our bodies and our clothes. This space is known as "ease."

The ease defines the overall fit of a garment. Even if a garment is shown in a particular fit, you may decide that you prefer something roomier or more snug. How do you know how much ease will give you a particular look or fit? There is a table, or fit chart, at www.yarnstandards.com, compiled by the Craft Yarn Council of America. It is based on the full bust measurement, not bra size. Measure yourself honestly and accurately to ensure a good fit.

Fit Chart

Very close-fitting	Actual chest/bust measurement or less
Close-fitting	1–2 inches (2.5–5 centimeters) greater than chest/bust
Standard-fitting	2–4 inches (5–10 centimeters) greater than chest/bust
Loose-fitting	4–6 inches (10–15 centimeters) greater than chest/bust
Oversized	6 inches (15 centimeters or more) greater than chest/bust

What this chart does not take into account is fabric thickness. When working with thinner, finer yarns, less ease is necessary. Conversely, when working with thicker, heavier yarns, more ease is necessary. This is because the thickness of the fabric "eats into" some of that space between you and the garment. It is the difference between the "inner circumference" versus the "outer circumference." Think of a car's tire, for instance. The inside circle is a lot smaller that the outside of the tire.

Opposite: Lily drapes a pattern directly on the body

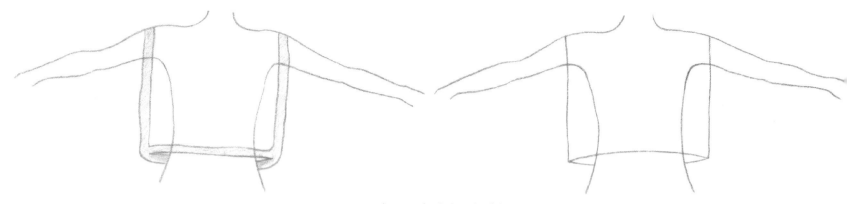

The ease of a thick vs thin fabric

I highly recommend the ease chart in Deborah Newton's *Designing Knitwear* (See Sources and Further Reading, page 159); fabric thickness is taken into consideration and the ease adjusted accordingly. Use this information not only in designing your own styles and determining the measurements you need to obtain these styles, but to decide on what size to make when following a pattern. Forget about the "labels" of Small, Medium, Large, etc. Don't think that you will always wear any one size. Instead, go by the numbers and look at the finished overall measurements. Ask yourself which set of numbers works best for what you have in mind.

Don't forget that the stitches that you use may alter the fabric's thickness. It's not just the yarn's diameter that determines thickness. Lacy stitches are considerably thinner than a solid fabric. Crocheted cables will thicken the fabric even more.

Sleeve Lengths and Neck Widths and Wrist Widths, Oh My!

If you've fitted a pattern for yourself (which I'm sure you mastered in Chapter 3!), you will have adjusted the lengths of the sleeves, perhaps the depth of the armholes. You will have figured out how wide a wrist opening is needed to accommodate your hands and what size neck hole will fit over your head. Furthermore, if there is any waist shaping, the narrowest part will have landed at the natural waist and not at the high hip.

But if you have never done this, if you're following a

pattern rather than designing your own, keep an eye on these key areas. Fashion may dictate that a high, tight neck is very *au courant,* but will you be able to pull it over your head? Use the measurements from a pattern, but make sure you compare them to yours.

Exactly how do you figure out how large a neck opening is, though? Transpose those schematic measurements onto square graph paper where each box is equal to 1 inch. Thus, the following set of schematics will look like the "before" and "after" illustrations on the next page.

Now take a piece of nonstretch yarn or string and follow the curve of the whole neckline, both front and back. This is how much that opening measures. I know, I know—your head is not that small! But since the square graph paper represents one inch, just straighten out that piece of yarn or string across some grid squares and count the total number of squares. That is, use the graph paper as your to-scale ruler.

Now, how much does your head measure at its fullest (including ears)? Does this pattern's neck measurement clear your head? If so, you're fine. If not, make a larger head hole by making a deeper front neck, a wider overall neck width, or a little of both. In real life, if using a full-size pattern, there are also flexible rulers that can measure around curves. Sewing notions and craft supply stores stock these rulers.

If you haven't fitted yourself (as per Chapter 3) and are following a pattern, you also need to know how to adjust your sleeve lengths. Measure yourself first from the center back neck (feel for the bone at the base of

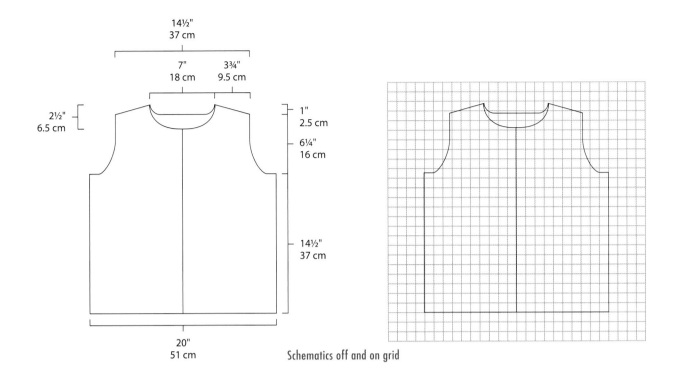

14½"
37 cm

7"
18 cm

3¾"
9.5 cm

2½"
6.5 cm

1"
2.5 cm

6¼"
16 cm

14½"
37 cm

20"
51 cm

Schematics off and on grid

your back neck) to your wrist, with your arm slightly down at a 45-degree angle (page 30, top).

My guess is that the range is from 26 to 34 inches. Now look at the schematic measurements to see what kind of center-back-to-wrist, or cbn-w, measurement is called for. In a drop-shouldered garment, that would be half the width of Back or Front plus Sleeve.

This set of schematics shows a cbn-w measurement of 30 inches (page 30, left side). If your cbn-w is less than this, shorten the sleeves until you achieve your own cbn-w. Conversely, if your cbn-w is more than this, lengthen the sleeves to get your own cbn-w. Of course, having lengthened or shortened a sleeve, you then have to address how to increase the sleeve width. You can't just go by what the directions say, but we'll deal with this in Chapter 5.

In a set-in sleeve, add up half the width of the back at the shoulder level, the height of the sleeve cap, then the rest of sleeve to arrive at the cbn-w measurement. In the example on the page 30, we get 27 inches. Again, if yours is more or less, make the adjustment in the sleeve length.

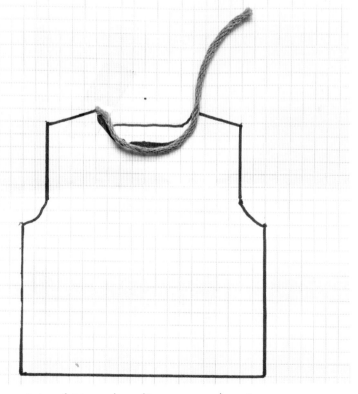

A piece of string can be used to measure a neck opening

Measure from the
base of your neck
to your wrist—
center-back-to-wrist
or cbn-w
measurement

20"
51 cm

20"
51 cm

Sample schematic for a
drop-shoulder garment

15"
38 cm

5"
12.5 cm

15"
38 cm

Schematic for a garment
with a set-in sleeve

Back Neck and Shoulder Shaping

These two little shapings may not be your favorite things to do. In fact, many dread the thought. However, incorporating them into a garment vastly improves the fit. Trust me, it's worth it. Garments all hang from the shoulders, the "hanger" that holds up the garment. Fit this area well and all else will follow.

If you take a look at the human anatomy, the head juts out forward and the neck is at an incline. Laws of gravity say that the neck then acts like a slide (see page 31). With a back neck that is straight across, garments will fall towards the back, thus hiking up the front and leaving you forever tugging on the front of your sweater.

Feel for the little hump or bone that protrudes slightly at the base of your neck. By "scooping out" about an inch's worth of fabric from the back neck, you clear that hump and the sweater will sit squarely on the shoulder. Don't just take my word for it. Take a look at any commercial garment—a T-shirt, sweatshirt, or any other top. It is a standard industry practice to add this back neck shaping. Even tops with collars—such as turtlenecks and blouses—feature it. Millions of manufacturers can't be wrong!

Let's talk about shoulder shaping. We are not built like linebackers. Our natural shoulders slope. The only exception to needing this slope in a garment is if large shoulder pads are inserted. And so we need to remove a bit of fabric at the top of the shoulders to accommodate this. If we don't, the fabric will fall and bunch up at the underarms, sometimes even extending down to the hemline (right). Unless you want batwing sleeves, take a tip from the industry pros and check out how often shoulder slopes are built into clothes that we buy. No matter how large or small the garment's body, it's important to shape shoulders for a proper fit.

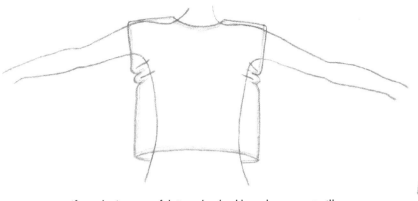

If you don't remove fabric at the shoulders, the garment will bunch up under the arms

Darts

Some of us are more well endowed than others. How do you know when you need (horizontal) bust darts? Tie a piece of yarn or string around mid-thigh. Drop a tape measure from the top of the shoulder (right next to the neck) down the back to where the yarn or string is and mark this length. From the same point at the high shoulder, drop the tape measure down the front over the full of the bust to mid-thigh. Write this number down. If the difference between the front and back is more than 2 inches, you probably need to add extra length to compensate for the, uh, shelf, since a full bust hikes up a fabric in front.

Horizontal bust darts, via short rows, are the usual solution. This gives extra length in the fabric that covers the center of the front and occurs right at the bustline. The sides of the front remain shorter and are the same length as the back. In sewing, excess fabric is removed by stitching down this dart. In crocheting, more fabric is inserted into the middle by having extra rows of work. This will work well for a simple stitch, but be warned that more involved stitch patterning may be interrupted. Since this extra work falls at the bust, it can be conspicuous at times. (Chapter 5 offers another solution.)

Vertical darts are when you draw in for the waist, typically via decreased stitches. This can create the illusion of a waist, even if you don't have one. Most anyone can benefit from some kind of waist shaping. It makes for a very flattering silhouette.

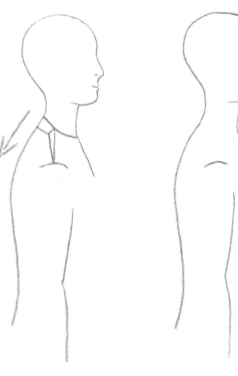

When designing garments, take into consideration head and neck

If the difference between front and back is more than 2 inches, add extra length to compensate for the bustline

Fabrication

When talking about refined fit, don't overlook the fabric itself. How often has crochet been accused of being stiff and bulky, like you're wearing an afghan? One way to alleviate this is to get a fabric with better drape. As addressed in Chapter 1, steam blocking can alter a fabric's drape for the better.

Other things that will influence the way a crocheted fabric drapes are the **stitches** (lacy ones are drapier than solid ones, taller ones are drapier than shorter ones, going through the front loops of all stitches makes for a drapier fabric than going through both loops of all stitches); **yarn thickness** (thicker ones are not as pliable as thinner ones); **yarn type** or **yarn**

construction (mohair does not drape as well as rayon or silk, woolen spun wool has less movement than worsted spun or combed wool, single-plied yarns are stiffer than multi-plied ones); **tension** (loosened gauges hang better than tighter ones), and so forth. How do you ultimately know the drape and other characteristics of the yarn and pattern you are working with? You don't need a fortune-teller: the swatch tells all.

For this reason, I tend towards the finer yarns that work with hook sizes C through F or G. Fear not the small gauges! Think about a fine, machine-knit sweater. It no doubt feels and looks better than that chunky rope that just about adds twenty pounds (and weighs a lot on its own). Take the time to make something worthy of your hands and your effort. Think in terms of quality, not quantity. It may take a little longer, but it will fit and feel and look that much better.

Of course, you sometimes want body and a bit of stiffness in a garment. In a coat, for instance, this is advantageous. The key is in matching the fabric to the project. Just as in sewing, where a pattern includes a list of recommended fabrics, crocheting should suggest fabric choices. A lot of it is common sense, however. Would you make a pair of overalls in chiffon? Conversely, a camisole in corduroy does not sound appealing or attractive. Ask yourself what type of fabric will bring the best out of a garment. What do you expect from the fabric of a shawl? A skirt? A jacket? Plotting out your garment before ever picking up a crochet hook will go a long way to ensuring that you will create a garment that makes you feel like the most clever and talented of designers!

A light slip works well under a crocheted dress or skirt. Buy several in complementary or contrasting colors.

FIVE

Crochet-Specific Stitching

Having come up with measurements and even a flat pattern that will fit, how
do we make the leap and translate these dimensions into crochet?
As a teenager, I did it instinctively by holding my work up to the shapes
I needed. Here are some more specific and precise approaches,
if you'd rather not fly by the seat of your pants.

Straightforward Crocheting

Where there is a solid "grid" of stitches, such as all single-crochet or all double-crochet, or even alternating rows of single and double crochet (as in my Positive/Negative Twin Set, page 55), knitting software can be a tremendous help to breaking a design down into numbers. Don't get scared off by the numbers. These are pretty simple calculations, I promise. If the gauge is 3 stitches and 4 rows per inch and you want a 20-inch-wide Back for your sweater, that's 20 x 3 = 60 stitches to begin with. If I'm not working in the round, I actually factor in 2 extra stitches, one on each side, as selvedges that get "eaten" up by the seaming. If the garment measures 25 inches long, 4 x 25 =100 rows total. Easy, right?

This is where many patterns stop, which results in boxy garments with a poor fit, not to mention a sad reputation for crochet.

The tricky part is doing the shaping. Without the help of computer programs or a flat pattern to measure against, let me recommend charting. Sleeve increase, armhole shaping, neck shaping, shoulder shaping—these can all be figured out visually on paper rather than mathematically (for the numbers-impaired . . .).

For the sleeve, if you know you need to increase 20 stitches over the course of 72 rows, the increases are divided equally at each side edge of the sleeve. Thus, you really need only 10 stitches at each side. I like to use gridded boxes where each grid represents a horizontal stitch and a vertical row. Do not confuse the *stitch* chart (where those *square* boxes represent inches) with the schematic measurements. In fact, each of the square boxes of your schematic measurements have 3 tiny stitches and 4 little rows—the equivalent of 1 inch—fitted into that square box, and that's what gauge really means.

For a more proportional picture, aim for graph paper that's closer to the desired gauge. There are websites to download such variable grids. There's also software called Print-A-Grid, which will generate true matches of your gauge. I personally use Stitch Painter from Cochenille. (See Sources and Further Reading, page 159.) It, too, has a variable grid that I can set.

Tape a few sheets of graph paper together if you must to get the necessary number of boxes. In our sleeve example, that's 10 boxes wide to represent our increased stitches and 72 boxes high to represent our total rows.

Having mapped out these "coordinates," just draw a line with red pencil from the beginning to where you

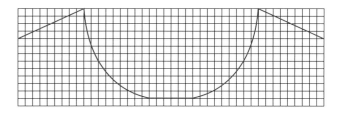

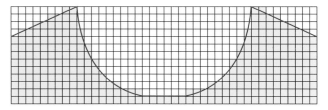

Neck and shoulder charting in 2 steps

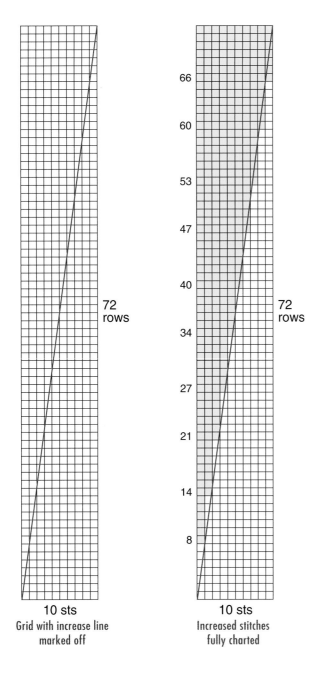

72 rows

10 sts
Grid with increase line
marked off

66

60

53

47

40

72 rows

34

27

21

14

8

10 sts
Increased stitches
fully charted

want to be at the end to determine how much increasing has to be done (far left).

Then fill in those boxes using the red increase line as a guide for those stitches gained in shaping the sleeve (of course, increase at the other edge as well). See left, middle.

Now you can modify your sleeve increases when changing sleeve lengths to cater to your own body's measurements. Are we having fun yet? The neck and the shoulder slope can follow a very similar process. Take a look at the charts above where the neck is 8 inches wide (or 24 stitches) and 3 inches deep (or 12 rows), and the shoulders are 3 inches wide (or 9 stitches) and the slope is 1 inch deep (or 4 rows).

If even this is more math than you want to handle, go totally "full scale" or life-size. Get a real neckline off an existing garment or draw the schematic measurements true to scale on gridded flip-chart paper and lay down the neckline over a true-to-gauge grid (one where the boxes are exactly the same size as your crocheting will be). Then just trace the neckline onto the gridded paper and follow the same procedure of filling in the boxes to represent the stitches. Now there's no need to even figure out how many stitches wide and how many rows long things are; you can physically see it in front of you (opposite).

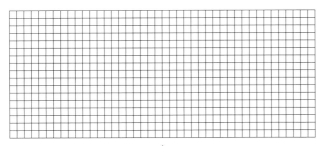

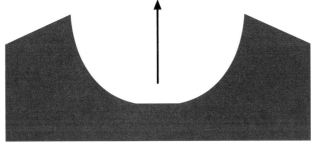

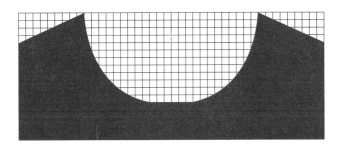

Neckline template over gridded paper

Shaping in Stitch Patterning

Using a more involved stitch that breaks away from those straight up-and-downs and side-to-sides presents a bigger challenge. How often have you worked a fancy lace pattern with a 7-stitch repeat, for instance, but became stumped when it came time to make refinements of fewer than 7 stitches? How do you shape the neckline? What do you do if you want a classic set-in sleeve instead of a drop shoulder? How can you create a refined fit and nip in for the waist while allowing for the bust? The answers lie within the stitch structure of a fancy pattern. Here are some of my trade secrets from my ready-to-wear experience.

To begin with, rather than dealing with a number of stitches per 4 inches or even per 1 inch, think in terms of pattern repeats. How much does each pattern repeat measure? Let's say a full shell pattern equals 1.5 inches. If you want a sweater back to measure 20 inches, 13 shells = 19.5 inches while 14 shells = 21 inches, so you'd have to pick from one of these choices in order to maintain full patterns. If not, there will be partial shells at either end. It helps a great deal to think in terms of full pattern repeats throughout.

There are basically five ways to incorporate shaping in a more complex pattern, in order from easiest to most difficult:

• Change hook size
• Change stitch heights
• Use plain filler stitches when shaping
• Work around stitch-pattern shapes
• Alter stitch pattern

Changing the hook size alters the gauge. It is a good way to narrow a piece in order to shape for the waist. Make gauge swatches in differing hook sizes to see exactly how big the piece will be using that particular hook. In a pinch, using a different hook size than what the pattern's gauge calls for is a down and dirty way of altering a size. Again, knowing what the new gauge is will tell you exactly how different the dimensions will be overall. Be aware that there are some limitations. Too tight a gauge can render a fabric as stiff as cardboard. Too loose a gauge can result in sleazy gauze.

Changing the stitch height is a good way to shape for bust darts and shoulder slopes. Use longer stitches for the area higher up at the shoulder, closer to the neck. Pictured on page 36 (top, right) is a shoulder slope comprised solely of single, half-double, double, and treble crochets rather than "binding off" in stair steps.

In lieu of short rows for a horizontal bust dart, use the longer stitches over the portion of the bust in the center of the fabric. Pictured on page 36 (left) is a lace pattern made up of double crochets at the side but treble crochets in the middle.

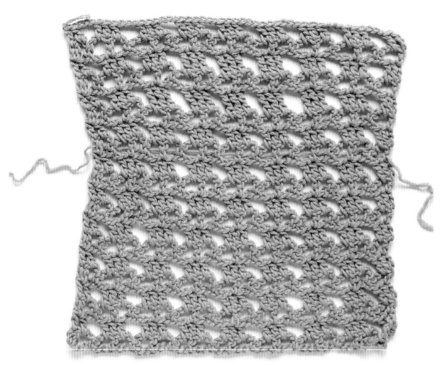

Swatch showing bust dart shaping via longer and shorter stitches

Swatch showing shoulder shaping via longer/shorter sts

Swatch showing shoulder shaping via stitching down the fabric

The cheat method for either shoulder slopes or horizontal darts is to emulate sewing and actually stitch the fabric down. This creates a bit more bulk and may be seen through lacier stitches, but won't require jumping through hoops. For a shoulder, either machine sew or hand-backstitch the diagonal line with the wrong sides facing out and with the right sides "kissing" to the insides. (See image at right.) The extra 1 inch of fabric near the arms can then be tacked down on the wrong side to form mini built-in shoulder pads.

If increasing stitches for the sleeve in the pattern proves too daunting, use what I call "filler stitches," or plain stitches of the same height as that of the pattern. When there are enough stitches to form a new pattern repeat, change over. In the swatch on page 37 (left) rows of double crochet are used for the increased portion.

Areas such as a sleeve cap, an armhole, and the neck can often be worked around the stitch patterns them-selves. That is, see if the lines of the pattern follow the lines of the desired shapes. To do this, make a good-size swatch of at least 8 x 8 inches (page 37, left, top). Make a few photocopies of this swatch to get a "working copy" on which to draw and make notes. Then lay a life-size template for the neck/armhole/sleeve cap over this photocopy (page 37, right, bottom).

Move the template piece around until you get a good line-up of stitches that jive with the template; draw the outlines onto the photocopy with a marker.

Increases via use of double crochet filler stitches

Photocopy of swatch with neckline drawn onto it

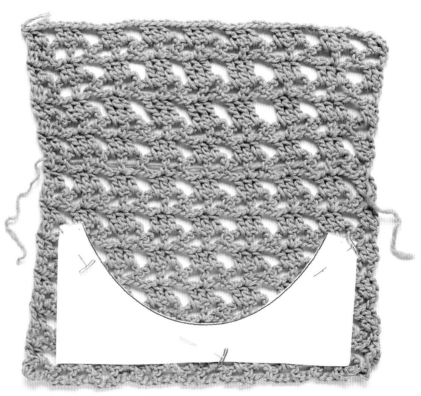

Neck template laid over swatch

This is very much like the image on page 37 (top, right) but instead of drawing over a rigid grid, the template is drawn over actual stitches in the pattern.

Smooth over some of the edges and make notes on where to end the stitch patterns. There is a great deal of room to fudge. Certain curves can be altered slightly to follow the stitch pattern. These curved shapes are not written in stone. You now have a map or blueprint to follow when crocheting the actual piece. It's almost like playing paper dolls! This also tells you how to initially center your stitch pattern, so the neck is easier to shape later.

Take this idea of a paper mock-up even further. Tape several pieces of the photocopied swatches together, lining up the stitch pattern repeats, until you have a paper version of the garment large enough to fit you. Without having to do any math whatsoever (except for basic counting), see how many pattern repeats you need for the full-size garment. You can plan all the shapings on this full-size paper mock-up as well.

Drawing the full stitch chart (opposite) is another way of mapping out the shaping. This supplements the marked-up photocopy.

Sometimes, when all else fails, the actual stitch pattern has to be altered. One of the easiest examples is the classic shell pattern of [sc, 5 dc, sc] that's the basis of Chapter 9. If some narrowing is desired, scatter a few [sc, 3 dc, sc] smaller shells across a given row. This would work well for some waist shaping. To widen, try a few shells of [sc, 7 dc, sc]. This would work well for a flared peplum, for instance. In the lace dress from Chapter 8, the use of three different-size variations of the fan shell helps shape the full, flared skirt. You have to get to know the pattern intimately in order to mess with its structure.

As a last resort, remember that blocking covers up a multitude of sins (see Chapter 1), and a trim of any kind can gloss over any irregular edges.

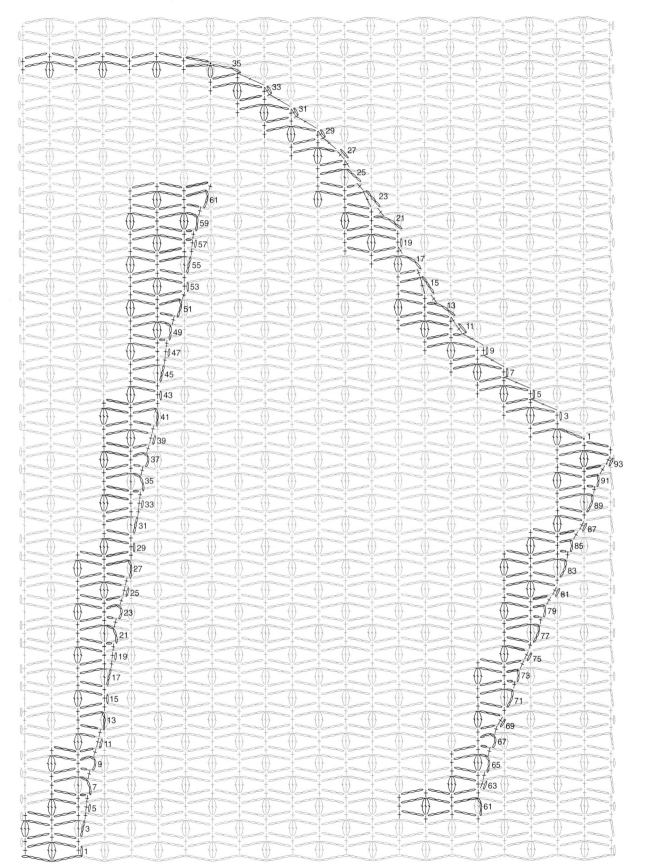

Full stitch chart of shaping

SIX

Simpler Stitches

These projects require just the basic stitches in a solid fabric, primarily in the rigid grid of stitch over stitch. Shaping is pretty straightforward.

Suits Me Jacket and Skirt

The top and bottom of a suit can coordinate but need not be an exact match. Raised stitches via front-post double-crochet stitches emphasize the princess "seam" lines in both jacket and skirt. Note how the ones on the skirt underscore the godet, or gusset, shapes. Follow the supplied color chart or switch up colors on the jacket spontaneously as you work.

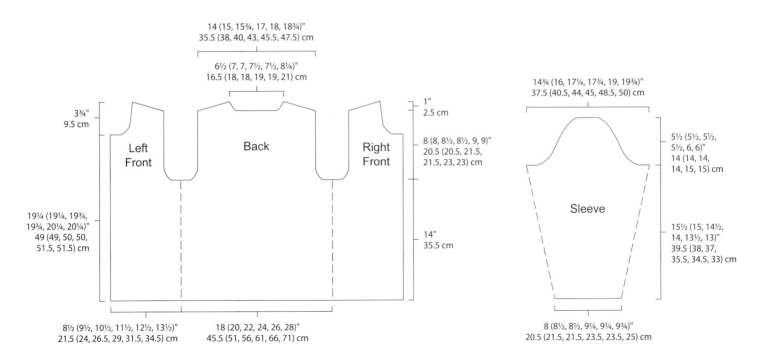

14 (15, 15¾, 17, 18, 18¾)"
35.5 (38, 40, 43, 45.5, 47.5) cm

6½ (7, 7, 7½, 7½, 8¼)"
16.5 (18, 18, 19, 19, 21) cm

14¾ (16, 17¼, 17¾, 19, 19¾)"
37.5 (40.5, 44, 45, 48.5, 50) cm

3¾"
9.5 cm

1"
2.5 cm

Left Front

Back

Right Front

8 (8, 8½, 8½, 9, 9)"
20.5 (20.5, 21.5, 21.5, 23, 23) cm

5½ (5½, 5½, 5½, 6, 6)"
14 (14, 14, 14, 15, 15) cm

Sleeve

19¼ (19¼, 19¾, 19¾, 20¼, 20¼)"
49 (49, 50, 50, 51.5, 51.5) cm

14"
35.5 cm

15½ (15, 14½, 14, 13½, 13)"
39.5 (38, 37, 35.5, 34.5, 33) cm

8½ (9½, 10½, 11½, 12½, 13½)"
21.5 (24, 26.5, 29, 31.5, 34.5) cm

18 (20, 22, 24, 26, 28)"
45.5 (51, 56, 61, 66, 71) cm

8 (8½, 8½, 9¼, 9¼, 9¾)"
20.5 (21.5, 21.5, 23.5, 23.5, 25) cm

Jacket

Finished Size

Sizes S (M, L, 1X, 2X, 3X): 36 (40, 44, 48, 52, 56)" (91.5 [101.5, 112, 122, 132, 142] cm) bust/chest circumference. This is a loose-fitting garment. Sample is worked in size M.

Materials

Yarn: Karabella Aurora 8 (100% extra-fine merino wool, 98 yd [90 m]/50 g): #11 olive (MC), 14 (14, 15, 17, 18, 20) skeins; #2 wine (W), #9 purple (P), #705 squash (S), and #1364 beige (B), 1 skein each.

Crochet Hook: Size I/9 (5.5 mm) for jacket. Size G/6 (4 mm) for buttons. Adjust hook size if necessary to obtain the correct gauge.

Notions: Smooth, contrast-color yarn to act as markers.

Gauge

13 sc and 15 sc rows = 4" (10 cm). This is a "hung" gauge. That is, measure with swatch hanging on a corkboard or pinned to towel on rack. Gravity will pull the rows a little longer than when measured flat.

Notes

- Body is worked in one piece up to the underarms. Sleeves are worked circularly in rnds up to the cap.
- When working with accent colors, crochet over MC. Chart shown is for size M; use as guideline for accent colors for other sizes or randomly create your own.

Special Stitches

Fpdc (front post double crochet): Yo, insert hook from front to back to front again around the post of next corresponding st 2 rows below, (yo, draw yarn through 2 loops on hook) twice to complete fpdc.

To "bind off" sts: At beg of row, sl st over stated number of sts, then sl st into next st to begin resuming work. At end of row, skip stated number of sts and do not work them.

Row 1 (RS): With MC and larger hook, loosely ch 116 (128, 140, 156, 168, 180), sc in 2nd ch from hook and in each ch across—115 (127, 139, 155, 167, 179) sc.

Row 2 (WS): Ch 1 and turn, begin Color Chart beg with Row 2 and sc in each sc across, joining accent colors as necessary and ending them off when through.

Row 3 (establish fpdc "princess seam" pattern): Ch 1 and turn, cont Color Chart and sc in first 12 (13, 14, 15, 16, 17) sc, * fpdc into each of the sc's 2 rows below next 2 sc, skip these 2 sc's that fpdc has now substituted for *, **sc in each of next 14 (16, 18, 21, 23, 25) sc, place contrasting yarn marker to mark "side seam," sc in each of next 14 (16, 18, 21, 23, 25) sc **, rep from * to *, sc in each of next 27 (29, 31, 33, 35, 37) sc, rep from * to *, rep from ** to **, rep from * to *, sc in each of last 12 (13, 14, 15, 16, 17) sc. Cont to carry "side seam" markers to aid in following Color Chart.

Row 4: Ch 1 and turn, cont Color Chart and sc in each sc across.

Row 5: Ch 1 and turn, cont Color Chart and sc in each sc across but work fpdc into each fpdc 2 rows below at each of 4 "princess seams."

Rep Rows 4 and 5 until piece measures 14" (35.5 cm) from beg, ending with a WS row.

Shape Right Front Armhole

With RS facing, cont Color Chart and work across first 26 (28, 30, 32, 35, 36) sts only, ending at armhole edge, turn. Dec at armhole edge every row 2 times, then every other row 3 (3, 4, 4, 5, 5) times. Work even on rem 21 (23, 24, 26, 28, 29) sts until armhole measures 5 1/4 (5 1/4, 5 3/4, 5 3/4, 6 1/4, 6 1/4)" (13.5 [13.5, 14.5, 14.5, 16, 16] cm) total.

Shape Right Front Neck

From neck edge, bind off 2 (3, 3, 4, 4, 4) sts on next row, then bind off 2 (2, 2, 2, 2, 3) st on foll row—17 (18, 19, 20, 22, 22) sts.

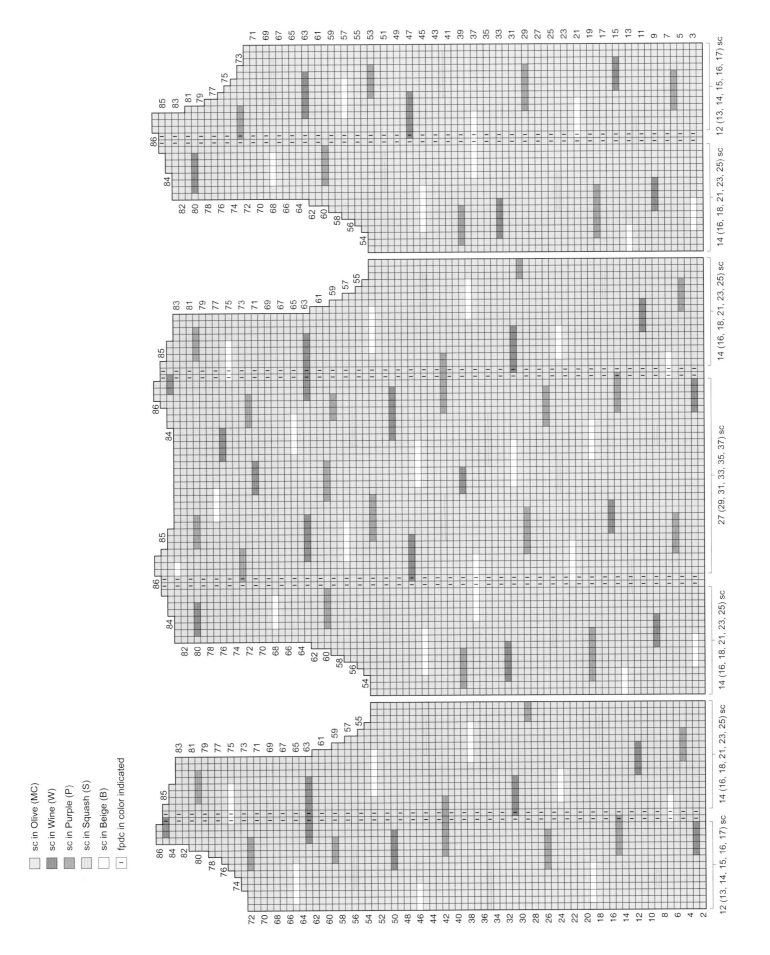

sc in Olive (MC)

sc in Wine (W)

sc in Purple (P)

sc in Squash (S)

sc in Beige (B)

fpdc in color indicated

Dec 1 st from each neck edge on next 3 rows, then every other row once, then every 3rd row once—12 (13, 14, 15, 17, 17) sts.

Shape Right Shoulder

AT THE SAME TIME, when armholes measure 8 (8, 8½, 8½, 9, 9)" (20.5 [20.5, 21.5, 21.5, 23, 23] cm), bind off from armhole edge 3 (4, 4, 4, 4, 4) sts on next row, 3 (3, 3, 3, 4, 4) sts on foll row, and 3 (3, 3, 4, 4, 4) sts on foll row—3 (3, 4, 4, 5, 5) sts rem. Fasten and end off.

Shape Back Armholes

With RS facing, skip next 4 (6, 8, 12, 12, 16) sts past first row of Right Front Armhole and join in next st, ch 1, cont Color Chart and sc in same st as join and in next 54 (58, 62, 66, 72, 74) sts for 55 (59, 63, 67, 73, 75) sts total. Shape as for Right Front Armhole at both ends.

Work even on 45 (49, 51, 55, 59, 61) sts until armholes measure 8 (8, 8½, 8½, 9, 9)" (20.5 [20.5, 21.5, 21.5, 23, 23] cm).

Shape Back Neck and Shoulders

Bind off from each armhole edge 3 (4, 4, 4, 4, 4) sts on next row, 3 (3, 3, 3, 4, 4) sts on foll row, and 3 (3, 3, 4, 4, 4) sts on foll row.

AT THE SAME TIME, bind off center 13 (15, 15, 17, 17, 19) sts, work rem sts. Join separate ball of yarn to other shoulder. Working both shoulders at the same time, bind off 3 sts from each neck edge once, then dec at neck edge once—3 (3, 4, 4, 5, 5) sts rem in each shoulder. Fasten and end off.

Shape Left Front

With RS facing, skip next 4 (6, 8, 12, 12, 16) sts past first row of Back Armhole and join in next st, ch 1, cont Color Chart and sc in same st as join and in rem sts.

Work as for Right Front, reversing all shaping. Fasten and end off.

Sleeves

With MC and larger hook, loosely ch 26 (28, 28, 30, 30, 32). Join with sl st to first ch to form circle, being careful not to twist.

Rnd 1: (RS) Ch 1, following Color Chart, sc in each ch around, join with sl st to first sc—26 (28, 28, 30, 30, 32) sc. Mark center 2 sts.

Cont in patt as described below, and inc 1 st at beg and end of every other rnd 0 (0, 0, 0, 1, 3) times, every 3 rnds 0 (0, 6, 9, 15, 13) times, every 4 rounds 2 (9, 8, 5, 0, 0) times, then every 5 rounds 9 (3, 0, 0, 0, 0) times, as follows: sc in 1st sc, work 2 sc's into 2nd sc, work in patt to last 2 sc's, work 2 sc's into next sc, sc in last sc.

Rnd 2: (WS) Ch 1 and turn, cont Color Chart and sc in each sc around, join with sl st to first sc.

Rnd 3 (establish fpdc pattern): Ch 1 and turn, cont Color Chart and sc to center 2 sts, fpdc into each of the sc's 2 rows below next 2 sc, skip these 2 sc's that fpdc has now substituted for, sc in each of rem sc.

Row 4: Ch 1 and turn, cont Color Chart and sc in each sc across.

Row 5: Ch 1 and turn, cont Color Chart and sc in each sc across but work fpdc into each fpdc 2 rows below.

Rep Rows 4 and 5. Complete sleeve inc's, then work even on 48 (52, 56, 58, 62, 64) sts until sleeves measure 15½ (15, 14½, 14, 13½, 13)" (39.5 [38, 37, 35.5, 34.5, 33] cm) from beg, ending with a WS row.

Shape Cap

Cont Color Patt and bind off 2 (3, 4, 6, 6, 8) sts from each end on next row.

Working back and forth in rows, dec at each edge every row 3 (7, 3, 2, 2, 2) times, then every other row 6 (5, 6, 7, 8, 8) times, then every row 4 (2, 4, 3, 3, 2) times. Bind off 2 sts from each end on next row—14 (14, 18, 18, 20, 20) sts rem. Fasten and end off.

Finishing

Block pieces to measurements. Sew shoulder seams. Set in sleeves.

Button Band

With RS facing, MC, and larger hook, sc evenly spaced along Left Front Edge. Work another 4 more rows of sc, fasten, and end off. Mark for 7 buttons evenly spaced.

Buttonhole Band

With RS facing, MC, and larger hook, sc same number of sts evenly spaced as for Button Band. Work another row of sc.

Row 3 (buttonhole row): Sc across and for each marked button of corresponding Button Band, ch 2, skip 2 sc.

Row 4: Sc across in each sc and in each ch of ch-2 buttonholes.

Row 5: Sc across. Fasten and end off.

Buttons: make 2 P, 2 S, 2 W, and 1 B.

Do not join rounds but mark them with piece of contrasting yarn. Make slipknot with about 4–6" (10–15 cm) tail; keep tail in FRONT of work at all times.

Rnd 1: (WS faces always) With smaller hook, ch 2, work 6 sc in 2nd ch from hook.

Rnd 3: Sc in each sc around.

Rnd 4: Sc in every OTHER sc around—6 sc.

Rnd 5: Slip st in every OTHER sc around—3 sl st.

Fasten and end off yarn, leaving 4–6" (10-15 cm) tail. Tie both beg and end tails tightly tog in square knot. Tie ends of buttons to each marked space of Button Band.

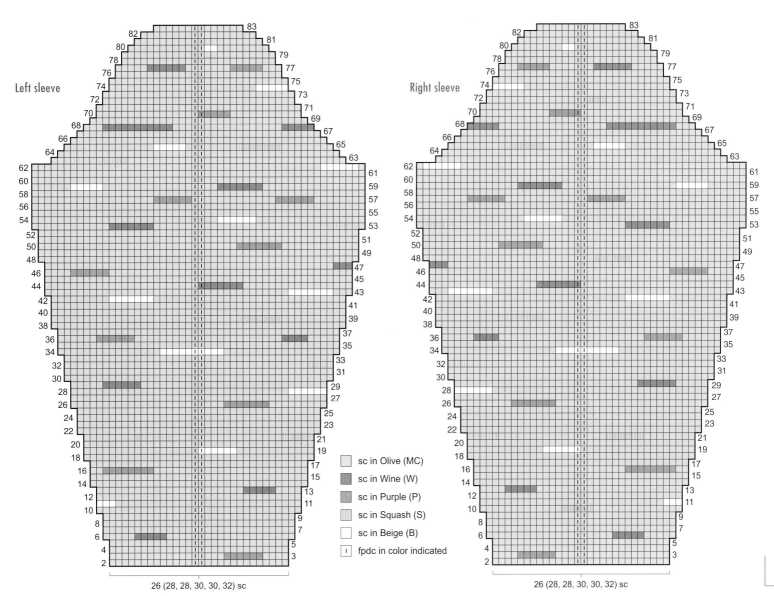

Left sleeve

Right sleeve

☐ sc in Olive (MC)
▨ sc in Wine (W)
▨ sc in Purple (P)
▥ sc in Squash (S)
☐ sc in Beige (B)
▐ fpdc in color indicated

26 (28, 28, 30, 30, 32) sc

26 (28, 28, 30, 30, 32) sc

Collar

With RS facing, MC, and larger hook, sc into side of first 2 rows of Buttonhole Band, sc 15 (16, 16, 17, 17, 18) sts evenly spaced around Right Front Neck, sc 23 (25, 25, 27, 27, 29) sts evenly spaced across Back Neck, sc 15 (16, 16, 17, 17, 18) sts evenly spaced around Left Front Neck, sc into side of first 2 rows of Button Band—57 (61, 61, 65, 65, 69) sts.

Work another 2 rows of sc.

Row 4 (RS): Ch 1 and turn, sc in first sc, *fpdc into the sc 2 rows below next sc, skip this sc that fpdc has now substituted for, sc in next sc; rep from * across.

Row 5 and all odd-numbered rows: Ch 1 and turn, sc in each st across.

Row 6: Ch 1 and turn, 2 sc in first sc, **fpdc into fpdc 2 rows below next st, skip this sc that fpdc has now substituted for *, sc in next sc, rep from * to *, 2 sc in next sc **; rep from ** to **—72 (77, 77, 82, 82, 87) sts.

Row 8: Ch 1 and turn, sc in each sc across and fpdc into each fpdc 2 rows below.

Row 10: Ch 1 and turn, sc in each of first 2 sc, **fpdc into fpdc 2 rows below next st, skip this sc that fpdc has now substituted for *, 2 sc in next sc, rep from * to *, sc in each of next 2 sc **; rep from ** to **—86 (92, 92, 98, 98, 104) sts.

Rows 12, 14, and 16: Ch 1 and turn, sc in each sc across and fpdc into each fpdc 2 rows below.

Work an extra sc at last st, rotate piece and sc evenly along one side of collar, sc along remaining Buttonhole Band rows, sl st in each st of Buttonhole Band, sc evenly along bottom edge of Body, sl st in each st of Button Band, sc along remaining Button Band rows, sc along other side of collar, join to beg of last Collar row worked, fasten and end off.

Skirt

Finished Size

25 (27½, 30, 32½, 35, 37½)" at (63.5 [70, 76, 82.5, 89, 95] cm) waist circumference. This garment is intended to be close-fitting. Skirt shown measures 27½" (70 cm).

Materials

Yarn: Karabella Vintage Cotton (100% mercerized cotton, 140 yd [130 m]/50 g): #306, deep purple, 9 (10, 11, 12, 13, 14) skeins.

Crochet hook: Size D/3 (3.25 mm). Adjust hook size if necessary to obtain the correct gauge.

Notions: One 7" (18 cm) matching zipper.

Sewing needle and matching sewing thread.

Smooth, contrast-color yarns for stitch markers.

Gauge

19 sts and 22 rows = 4" (10 cm) in patt. This is a "hung" gauge. That is, measure with swatch hanging on a corkboard or pinned to towel on rack. Gravity will pull the rows a little longer than when measured flat.

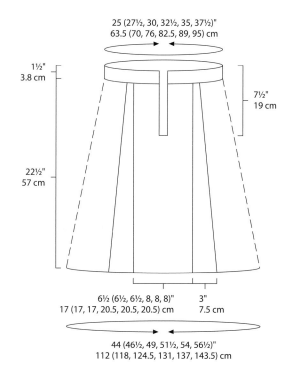

25 (27½, 30, 32½, 35, 37½)"
63.5 (70, 76, 82.5, 89, 95) cm

1½"
3.8 cm

7½"
19 cm

22½"
57 cm

6½ (6½, 6½, 8, 8, 8)"
17 (17, 17, 20.5, 20.5, 20.5) cm

3"
7.5 cm

44 (46½, 49, 51½, 54, 56½)"
112 (118, 124.5, 131, 137, 143.5) cm

Notes

- Skirt is worked seamlessly from top down. Many things are happening at once. Creating a full stitch chart using several sheets of graph paper taped together is strongly suggested.

Special Stitches

Fpdc (front post double crochet): Yo, insert hook from front to back to front again around the post of next corresponding st 2 rows below, (yo, draw yarn through 2 loops on hook) twice to complete fpdc.

Sc2tog (decrease one single crochet): [Pick up lp in next st] twice, yarn around hook and pull through rem 3 lps on hook.

Waistband

Loosely ch 115 (127, 139, 151, 163, 175).

Row 1: (RS) Sc in 2nd ch from hook and in each ch across—114 (126, 138, 150, 162, 174) sc.

Row 2 and ALL even rows: (WS) Ch 1 and turn, sc in each sc across.

Row 3 (establish "rib" patt of fpdc): Ch 1 and turn, sc in first sc, fpdc around the post of next corresponding sc in Row 1 directly below next st, sk sc behind fpdc just made, *sc in each of next 2 sc, fpdc around the post of next corresponding sc in Row 1 directly below next st, sk sc behind fpdc just made; rep from * across, ending with sc in last sc.

Row 4: Rep Row 2.

Row 5: Ch 1 and turn, sc in first sc, fpdc around the post of next corresponding fpdc 2 rows directly below next st, sk sc behind fpdc just made, *sc in each of next 2 sc, fpdc around the post of next correspon-

ding fpdc 2 rows directly below next st, sk sc behind fpdc just made; rep from * across, ending with sc in last sc.

Row 6: Rep Row 2.

Rows 7 and 8: Rep Rows 5 and 6. (Waistband should measure 1¹/₂" [3.8 cm] total). While working Row 8, with contrasting yarn, place a marker bet 14th and

15th (14th and 15th, 14th and 15th, 17th and 18th, 17th and 18th, 17th and 18th) sts for dart, bet 27th and 28th (30th and 31st, 33rd and 34th, 36th and 37th, 39th and 40th, 42nd and 43rd) sts for side "seam," bet 40th and 41st (46th and 47th, 52nd and 53rd, 55th and 56th, 61st and 62nd, 67th and 68th) sts for dart, bet 74th and 75th (80th and 81st, 86th and 87th, 95th and 96th, 101st and 102nd, 107th and 108th) sts for dart, bet 87th and 88th (96th and 97th, 105th and 106th, 114th and 115th, 123rd and 124th, 132nd and 133rd) sts for side "seam" and bet 100th and 101st (112th and 113th, 124th and 125th, 133rd and 134th, 145th and 146th, 157th and 158th) sts for dart.

Body

Row 1 (RS): Maintain all markers, ch 1 and turn, sc in first 13 (13, 13, 16, 16, 16) sc, *fpdc around the post of next corresponding fpdc 2 rows directly below next st and sk sc behind fpdc just made, sc in each of next 2 sc, fpdc around the post of next corresponding fpdc 2 rows directly below next st and sk sc behind fpdc just made*, **sc in each of next 8 (11, 14, 14, 17, 20) sc, 2 sc in next sc for inc, sc in each of next 2 sc, 2 sc in next sc for inc (there are now inc's 1 st from either side of side "seam" marker), sc in each of next 8 (11, 14, 14, 17, 20) sc**, rep from * to *, sc in each of next 32 (32, 32, 38, 38, 38) sc, rep from * to *, rep from ** to **, rep from * to *, sc in each of rem 13 (13, 13, 16, 16, 16) sc–118 (130, 142, 154, 166, 178) sts.
Cont to inc in same manner 1 st from either side of each side "seam" marker every 3 rows 6 more times, then every 5 rows twice while maintaining established fpdc patt.

AT THE SAME TIME, when work measures 2½" (6.5 cm) total, ending ready to work RS row, work interior dart inc's as follows: Maintaining est fpdc patt, *work in patt to first dart marker, inc by working sc in sc behind fpdc just worked, work to next dart marker, sc in next sc, then work fpdc over this same st for another inc*; rep from * to *, work in patt to end. Rep this inc every 6th row twice, every 8th row once, then every 10th row 9 times.

AT THE SAME TIME, when work measures 7½" (19 cm) total, join piece to form a tube and end zipper opening as follows: at end of last row, ch 6, join with sl st to first sc. From here on, always join rows with sl st to beg sc and cont to turn work at end of each rnd.

Work even in est patt, in joined rnds on 200 (212, 224, 236, 248, 260) sts until piece measures 24" (61 cm) from beg or to desired length (note that longer length may require more yarn), ending with a RS row.

Finishing
Block piece to measurement. With RS facing, sc evenly around zipper opening, working sc2tog at each inner corner. Sew in zipper.

Maiko Jacket

Maikos are geishas in training and they wear much plainer kimonos. In this garment, the textured and variegated yarn and shape add interest, as does the subtle stitch pattern. Close with a hairpin or ornament, or leave open. To see the stitches through the textured yarn, hold your work up to a light source (such as a lamp).

Finished Size

38 (42, 46, 50, 54, 58)" (96.5 [106.5, 117, 127, 137, 147.5] cm) bust/chest circumference. This garment is intended to be over-size. Jacket shown measures 42" (106.5 cm).

Materials

Yarn: Lily Chin Signature Collection Nolita (26% wool, 21% acrylic, 48% polyester, 5% viscose, 98 yd [89 m]/50 g), #7312 chartreuse, 11 (12, 14, 15, 17, 18) skeins.

Crochet hook: Size K/10½ (6.5 mm). Adjust hook size if necessary to obtain the correct gauge.

Notions: Smooth, contrasting yarn as marker. Yarn needle.

Gauge

12 sts and 8 rows = 4" (10 cm) in patt when hung up.

Note

- Bottom pieces are worked separately, then joined. Upper torso is worked in one piece, then separated at underarms. Fronts and Back are worked back and forth in rows. Shoulder shaping occurs only on front shoulder pieces. Sleeves are worked circularly in the round up to the cap, then cap is worked in rows.

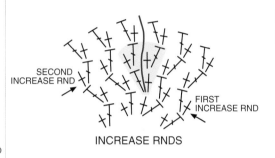

INCREASE RNDS

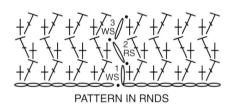

PATTERN IN RNDS

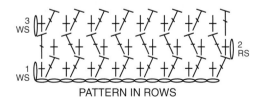

PATTERN IN ROWS

Special Stitches

First Inc Rnd (see chart): Work up to marked center completing exactly half the number of sts of previous rnd, in next sc, work sc, place yarn marker, work dc in same sc, complete row in patt—2 more sts in row than previous rnd. Note that center yarn marker winds up between sc and dc from here on.

Second Inc Rnd (see chart): Work up to dc before marked center, [sc and dc] all in next dc, place yarn marker, [sc and dc] all in next sc, complete row in patt—2 more sts in row than previous rnd. Note that center yarn marker winds up between dc and sc from here on.

Bind off sts at beg of row by working designated number of sl sts; at end of row by not working designated number of sts.

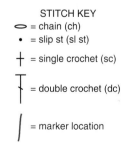

STITCH KEY

- ⬭ = chain (ch)
- • = slip st (sl st)
- + = single crochet (sc)
- ⊤ = double crochet (dc)
- | = marker location

Body

Back Bottom

Loosely ch 58 (64, 70, 76, 82, 88).

Row 1: (WS) (Sc, dc) all in 2nd ch from hook, *skip next ch, (sc, dc) all in next ch; rep from * across—58 (64, 70, 76, 82, 88) sts.

Row 2: (RS) Ch 1 and turn, *(sc, dc) all in next dc, skip next sc; rep from * across to within last dc, sc in dc, dc in last sc.

Rep Row 2 and work even until piece measures 5½" (14 cm) from beg or 11 rows, ending with a WS row, fasten and end off.

Left Front Bottom

Loosely ch 18 (20, 22, 24, 26, 30).

Work as for Back Bottom until piece measures 3½" (9 cm) from beg or 7 rows, ending with a WS row, fasten and end off.

Right Front Bottom

Work as for Left Front Bottom, do not fasten and end off.

Join Body

With RS facing and still working Right Front Bottom, work across piece, ch 2, with RS of Back Bottom facing, work across these sts in patt, ch 2, with RS of Left Front Bottom facing, work across these sts in patt—94 (104, 114, 124, 134, 148) sts not including ch-2s and 98 (108, 118, 128, 138, 152) sts including ch-2s.

Next Row: Work in patt across, working (sc, dc) in first ch of each ch-2 space at sides—98 (108, 118, 128, 138, 152) sts.

Continue to work even in patt until piece meas 16" (40.5 cm) total in Back and 14" (35.5 cm) total in each Front, ending with a RS row.

Separate for Armholes/Left Front Armhole

With WS facing, continue in patt and work across first 14 (14, 14, 14, 16, 18) sts only, ending at armhole edge, turn.

Work even until armhole measures 8 (8, 8½, 8½, 9¼, 10)" (20.5 [20.5, 21.5, 21.5, 23.5, 25.5] cm) from beg of armhole shaping.

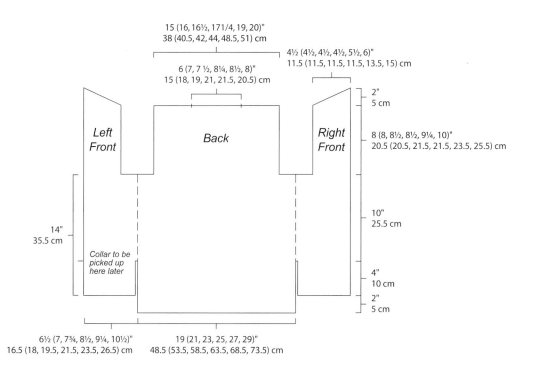

15 (16, 16½, 17¼, 19, 20)"
38 (40.5, 42, 44, 48.5, 51) cm

4½ (4½, 4½, 4½, 5½, 6)"
11.5 (11.5, 11.5, 11.5, 13.5, 15) cm

6 (7, 7½, 8¼, 8½, 8)"
15 (18, 19, 21, 21.5, 20.5) cm

2"
5 cm

Left Front

Back

Right Front

8 (8, 8½, 8½, 9¼, 10)"
20.5 (20.5, 21.5, 21.5, 23.5, 25.5) cm

10"
25.5 cm

14"
35.5 cm

Collar to be picked up here later

4"
10 cm

2"
5 cm

6½ (7, 7¾, 8½, 9¼, 10½)"
16.5 (18, 19.5, 21.5, 23.5, 26.5) cm

19 (21, 23, 25, 27, 29)"
48.5 (53.5, 58.5, 63.5, 68.5, 73.5) cm

Shape Shoulder

Work in patt, binding off 2 (2, 2, 2, 2, 4) sts from Shoulder edge on next row; then bind off 4 sts on next row; then bind off 2 sts on next row, then bind off 4 sts on next row—2 (2, 2, 2, 4, 4) sts rem, fasten and end off.

Back Armhole

With WS facing, skip next 12 (16, 20, 24, 24, 28) sts past first row of Left Front Armhole and join yarn in next dc, ch 1, (sc, dc) in same st as join and work even in patt until 46 (48, 50, 52, 58, 60) sts total have been completed, turn. Work even in patt until armhole measures 8 (8, 8½, 8½, 9¼, 10)" (20.5 [20.5, 21.5, 21.5, 23.5, 25.5] cm) from beg of armhole shaping, fasten and end off.

Right Front Armhole

With WS facing, skip next 12 (16, 20, 24, 24, 28) sts past first row of Back Armhole and join yarn in next st, ch 1, (sc, dc) in same st as join and work even in patt across—14 (14, 14, 14, 16, 18) sts.
Work even until armhole measures 8 (8, 8½, 8½, 9¼, 10)" (20.5 [20.5, 21.5, 21.5, 23.5, 25.5] cm) from beg of armhole shaping.

Sleeve (make 2)

Loosely ch 28 (28, 28, 32, 32, 32), join with sl st to first ch to form circle, being careful not to twist.

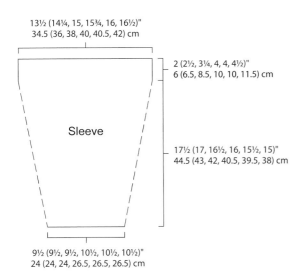

13½ (14¼, 15, 15¾, 16, 16½)"
34.5 (36, 38, 40, 40.5, 42) cm

2 (2½, 3¼, 4, 4, 4½)"
6 (6.5, 8.5, 10, 10, 11.5) cm

Sleeve

17½ (17, 16½, 16, 15½, 15)"
44.5 (43, 42, 40.5, 39.5, 38) cm

9½ (9½, 9½, 10½, 10½, 10½)"
24 (24, 24, 26.5, 26.5, 26.5) cm

Rnd 1 (WS): Ch 1, (sc, dc) all in first ch *skip next ch, (sc, dc) all in next ch; rep from * across, skip last ch, join with sl st to first sc.

Rnd 2: Ch 1 and turn, *(sc, dc) all in next dc, skip next sc; rep from * across placing yarn marker between sts 14 and 15 (14 and 15, 14 and 15, 16 and 17, 16 and 17, 16 and 17), join with sl st to first sc. From here on, carry yarn marker upwards to mark center.

Rep Rnd 2 for patt and cont to carry center yarn marker upwards and work First Inc Rnd, then Second Inc Rnd alternately as follows: Inc 2 sts every other rnd 0 (0, 6, 2, 8, 14) times, then inc 2 sts every 3rd rnd 10 (10, 6, 8, 4, 0) times.

Work even on 48 (48, 52, 52, 56, 60) sts until sleeves measures 17½ (17, 16½, 16, 15½, 15)" (44.5 [43, 42, 40.5, 39.5, 38] cm) from beg.

Cap

From here on, do not join but work in Rows as per Body by working last dc into last sc. Work even in patt until cap measures 2 (2½, 3¼, 4, 4, 4½)" (5 [6.5, 8.5, 10, 10, 11.5] cm), fasten and end off.

Finishing

Block pieces to measurements. Sew shoulder seams. Sew top of sleeves to armholes. Sew side edges of cap to skipped armhole sts.

Collar

With RS facing, skip bottom 4" (10 cm) of Right Front edge, join yarn and work 60 (60, 62, 62, 64, 66) sc evenly spaced along remainder of Right Front edge, work 20 (22, 24, 26, 28, 26) sc across Back Neck, then work 60 (60, 62, 62, 64, 66) sc evenly spaced along Left Front edge to within 4" (10 cm) of bottom edge—140 (142, 148, 150, 156, 158) sts total.
Work as for Body in patt st until Collar measures 6½ (7½, 8, 8¾, 9, 8¾)" (16.5 [19, 20.5, 22, 23, 22] cm), fasten and end off.

Positive/Negative Twin Set

A "twin set" does not always have to be a perfect match. Reversing the colors coordinates the pieces beautifully without getting that "matchy matchy" effect. A fine stitch gauge and fluid yarn means lots of drape, and the subtle stitch pattern is manageable and allows for a lot of refined shaping.

Cardigan

Finished Size
36 (40, 44, 48, 52, 56)" (91.5 [101.5, 112, 122, 132, 142] cm) bust/chest circumference. This garment is intended to be loose-fitting. Sweater shown measures 40" (101.5 cm).

Materials
Yarn: Berroco/Lang Opal (58% nylon, 42% viscose, 169 yd [155 m]/50 g): #0099 olive (O), 11 (12, 13, 14, 16, 17) skeins and #0063 wine (W), 2 (2, 2, 2, 2, 3) skeins.

Crochet hook: Size D/3 (3.25 mm). Adjust hook size if necessary to obtain the correct gauge.

Notions: Seven 7/8" (2.2 cm) buttons. Smooth, contrasting yarn for stitch markers.

Gauge
25 sts and 18 rows = 4" (10 cm) in patt (Alternating 1 row of dc and 1 row of sc) when steam-blocked.

Notes
- Body is worked in one piece up to the underarms. Sleeves are worked circularly in rnds up to the cap.

Special Stitches
Sc2tog (decrease one single crochet): [Pick up lp in next st] twice, yarn around hook and pull through rem 3 lps on hook.

Dc2tog (decrease one double crochet): [Yarn around hook, pick up lp in next st, yarn around hook and pull through 2 lps on hook] twice, yarn around hook and pull through rem 3 lps on hook.

To "bind off" sts: At beg of row, sl st over stated number of sts, then sl st in next st to begin resuming work. At end of row, skip stated number of sts and do not work them.

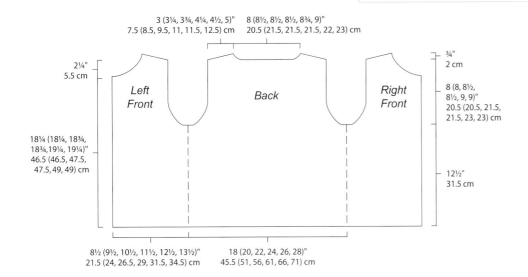

3 (3¼, 3¾, 4¼, 4½, 5)"
7.5 (8.5, 9.5, 11, 11.5, 12.5) cm

8 (8½, 8½, 8½, 8¾, 9)"
20.5 (21.5, 21.5, 21.5, 22, 23) cm

2¼"
5.5 cm

Left Front

Back

Right Front

¾"
2 cm

8 (8, 8½, 8½, 9, 9)"
20.5 (20.5, 21.5, 21.5, 23, 23) cm

18¼ (18¼, 18¾, 18¾, 19¼, 19¼)"
46.5 (46.5, 47.5, 47.5, 49, 49) cm

12½"
31.5 cm

8½ (9½, 10½, 11½, 12½, 13½)"
21.5 (24, 26.5, 29, 31.5, 34.5) cm

18 (20, 22, 24, 26, 28)"
45.5 (51, 56, 61, 66, 71) cm

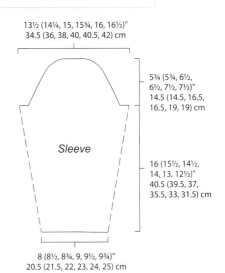

13½ (14¼, 15, 15¾, 16, 16½)"
34.5 (36, 38, 40, 40.5, 42) cm

5¾ (5¾, 6½, 6½, 7½, 7½)"
14.5 (14.5, 16.5, 16.5, 19, 19) cm

Sleeve

16 (15½, 14½, 14, 13, 12½)"
40.5 (39.5, 37, 35.5, 33, 31.5) cm

8 (8½, 8¾, 9, 9½, 9¾)"
20.5 (21.5, 22, 23, 24, 25) cm

Body

With O, loosely ch 222 (246, 271, 295, 322, 346).

Row 1 (RS): Sc in 2nd ch from hook and in each ch across—221 (245, 270, 294, 321, 345) sc.

Row 2 (WS): Ch 3 and turn (counts as a dc), sk first sc, dc in each each sc across—221 (245, 270, 294, 321, 345) dc.

Row 3: Ch 1 (does not count as a st) and turn, sc in each dc across—221 (245, 270, 294, 321, 345) sc.

Rep Rows 2 and 3 for patt. Cont to work in patt and mark bet st 54 (60, 66, 72, 79, 85) and st 55 (61, 67, 73, 80, 86) for one side "seam" and bet sts 167 (185, 204, 222, 242, 260) and st 168 (186, 205, 223, 242, 261) for other side "seam."

Work in est patt until piece measures 12½" (31.5 cm) total or 56 rows total.

Right Front Armhole

With RS facing, work across first 49 (54, 59, 64, 70, 75) sts only, ending at armhole edge, turn. Working across these sts only in patt, dec 1 st at armhole edge every row 4 (6, 8, 11, 13, 17) times, then dec 1 st at armhole edge every other row 2 (2, 2, 2, 2, 0) times, then dec 1 st at armhole edge every 3rd row 1 (1, 1, 0, 0, 0) time.

Work even on 42 (45, 48, 51, 55, 58) sts until armhole measures 5¾ (5¾, 6¼, 6¼, 6¾, 6¾)" (14.5 [14.5, 16, 16, 17, 17] cm).

Shape Neck

From neck edge, bind off 11 (12 12, 12, 13, 14) sts on next row, then bind off 3 st on next row, then dec 1 st every row 7 times, then dec 1 st every other row twice.

Shape Shoulders

AT THE SAME TIME, when armholes measures 8 (8, 8½, 8½, 9, 9)" (20.5 [20.5, 21.5, 21.5, 23, 23] cm), bind off from each shoulder edge: 5-4-5-5 (6-5-5-5, 6-6-6-6, 7-6-7-7, 8-7-7-8, 8-8-8-8). Fasten and end off.

Back Armhole

With RS facing, sk next 10 (12, 14, 16, 18, 20) sts past first row of Right Front Armhole and join in next st, maintaining est patt, work in same st as join and in next 102 (112, 123, 133, 144, 154) sts for 103 (113, 124, 134, 145, 155) sts total.

Shape as for Right Front Armhole at both ends. Work even on 89 (95, 102, 108, 115, 121) sts until armholes measures 8 (8, 8½, 8½, 9, 9)" (20.5 [20.5, 21.5, 21.5, 23, 23] cm).

Shape Back Neck and Shoulders

Work across first 24 (26, 29, 32, 35, 37) sts, sk next center 41 (43, 44, 44, 45, 47) sts, join separate ball of yarn to next st, work in same st as join and in next 23 (25, 28, 31, 34, 36) sts. Work both shoulders at same time with separate balls of yarn.

Bind off from each shoulder edge as for Right Front Shoulder. AT THE SAME TIME, bind off from each neck edge 3 sts, then dec 1 st at neck edge every row twice. Fasten and end off.

Left Front Armhole

With RS facing, sk next 10 (12, 14, 16, 18, 20) sts past first row of Back Armhole and join in next st, maintaining est patt, work in same st as join and in next 48 (53, 58, 63, 69, 74) sts for 49 (54, 59, 64, 70, 75) sts total.

Work as for Right Front reversing all shaping. Fasten and end off.

Sleeve

With O, loosely ch 51 (53, 55, 57, 59, 61), join with sl st to first ch to form circle, being careful not to twist.

Rnd 1 (RS): Ch 1 (does not count as a st), sc in each ch around—51 (53, 55, 57, 59, 61) sts, join with sl st to first sc.

Rnd 2 (WS): Ch 3 (counts as dc) and turn, sk first sc, dc in each sc around, join with sl st top of beg ch-3.

Size S: Work in est patt and inc at beg and end of row every 4th row 17 times—85 sts.

Size M: Work in est patt and inc at beg and end of row every 3rd row 6 times then every 4th row 12 times—89 sts.

Size L: Work in est patt and inc at beg and end of row every 3rd row 12 times then every 4th row 6 times—91 sts.

Size XL: Work in est patt and inc at beg and end of row every 3rd row 17 times then every 4th row 2 times—95 sts.

Size 2X: Work in est patt and inc at beg and end of row every 2nd row 2 times then every 3rd row 17 times—97 sts.

Size 3X: Work in est patt and inc at beg and end of row every 2nd row 7 times then every 3rd row 13 times—101 sts. Work even on 85 (89, 91, 95, 97, 101) sts until sleeve measures 16 (15½, 14½, 14, 13, 12½)" (40.5 [39.5, 37, 35.5, 33, 31.5] cm) from beg.

Shape Cap

Keeping to patt, bind off 5 (6, 7, 8, 9, 10) sts from each end on next row, dec 1 st at each end of every row 22 (20, 29, 27, 16, 16) times, at each end of every other row 0 (0, 0, 0, 6, 6) times, then bind off 2 sts from each end of every row 2 (5, 0, 2, 4, 3) times, then bind off 3 sts from each end of every row 1 (0, 0, 0, 0, 1) time—17 (17, 19, 17, 19, 19) sts rem, fasten and end off.

Finishing

Block pieces to measurements. Sew shoulder seams. Set in sleeves.

Bottom Trim

Row 1: With RS facing, working across opposite side of foundation ch, join W in first ch on bottom edge, ch 1, sc evenly across bottom edge.

Rows 2–5: Ch 1 and turn, sc in each sc across. At end of last row, fasten and end off.

Button Band

Row 1: With RS facing, join W at top corner of Left Front edge, ch 1, sc evenly along Left Front edge.

Rows 2–7: Ch 1 and turn, sc in each sc across. At end of last row, fasten and end off. Mark position for 6 buttons evenly spaced across Button Band with top button 2" (5 cm) below top neck edge and bottom button about 2¼" (5.5 cm) above bottom edge. Sew on buttons.

Buttonhole Band

Row 1: With RS facing, join W at bottom corner of Right Front edge, ch 1, sc evenly across Right Front edge.

Rows 2–3: Ch 1 and turn, sc in each sc across.

Buttonhole Row: Ch 1 and turn, sc evenly across, working ch 3, sk next 3 sc opposite each corresponding button on Button Band.

Row 5: Ch 1, sc in each sc across, working 3 sc in each ch-3 buttonhole loop.

Rows 6–7: Ch 1 and turn, sc in each sc across. At end of last row, fasten and end off.

Neckband

Row 1: With RS facing, join W in right-hand corner of neck edge, ch 1, sc evenly around neck edge.

Row 2: Ch 1 and turn, sc evenly across, working one buttonhole at Right Front about 2 sts in from edge.

Row 3: Ch 1, sc in each sc across, working 3 sc in ch-3 buttonhole loop.

Rows 4–5: Ch 1 and turn, sc in each sc across. At end of last row, fasten and end off. Sew rem button to buttonband opposite buttonhole.

Tank Top

Finished Size

33 (36, 39, 42, 45, 48)" (84 [91.5, 99, 106.5, 114.5, 122] cm) bust/chest circumference. This garment is intended to be close-fitting. Top shown measures 36" (91.5 cm).

Materials

Yarn: Berroco/Lang Opal (58% nylon, 42% viscose, 169 yd [155 m]/50 g): #0063 wine (W), 5 (6, 7, 10, 11) skeins and #0099 olive (O), 1 (1, 1, 1, 2) skeins.

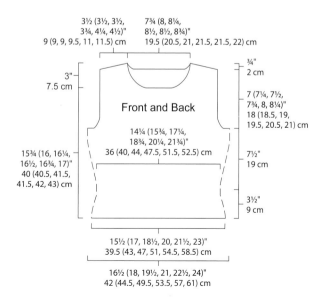

3½ (3½, 3½, 3¾, 4¼, 4½)"
9 (9, 9, 9.5, 11, 11.5) cm

7¾ (8, 8¼, 8½, 8½, 8¾)"
19.5 (20.5, 21, 21.5, 21.5, 22) cm

3"
7.5 cm

¾"
2 cm

7 (7¼, 7½, 7¾, 8, 8¼)"
18 (18.5, 19, 19.5, 20.5, 21) cm

Front and Back

14¼ (15¾, 17¼, 18¾, 20¼, 21¾)"
36 (40, 44, 47.5, 51.5, 52.5) cm

15¾ (16, 16¼, 16½, 16¾, 17)"
40 (40.5, 41.5, 41.5, 42, 43) cm

7½"
19 cm

3½"
9 cm

15½ (17, 18½, 20, 21½, 23)"
39.5 (43, 47, 51, 54.5, 58.5) cm

16½ (18, 19½, 21, 22½, 24)"
42 (44.5, 49.5, 53.5, 57, 61) cm

Crochet hook: Size D/3 (3.25 mm). Adjust hook size if necessary to obtain the correct gauge.

Notions: Smooth, contrasting yarn as st marker.

Gauge

25 sts and 18 rows = 4" (10 cm) in patt (alternating 1 row of sc and 1 row of dc) when steam-blocked.

Note

• Body is worked in rnds seamlessly with sl st joins at ends of rnds.

Special Stitches

Sc2tog (decrease one single crochet): [Pick up lp in next st] twice, yarn around hook and pull through rem 3 lps on hook.

Dc2tog (decrease one double crochet): [Yarn around hook, pick up lp in next st, yarn around hook and pull through 2 lps on hook] twice, yarn around hook and pull through rem 3 lps on hook.

To "bind off" sts: At beg of row, sl st over stated number of sts, then sl st in next st to begin resuming work. At end of row, skip stated number of sts and do not work them.

Body

With W, loosely ch 194 (214, 232, 250, 270, 288), join with sl st to first ch to form circle, being careful not to twist.

Rnd 1 (RS): Ch 1 (does not count as a st), sc in each ch around, join with sl st to first sc—194 (214, 232, 250, 270, 288) sc.

Rnd 2 (WS): Ch 3 and turn (counts as a dc), sk first sc, dc in each sc around, join with sl st to top of beg ch—194 (214, 232, 250, 270, 288) dc.

Rnd 3: Ch 1 (does not count as a st) and turn, sc in each dc around, join with sl st to first sc—194 (214, 232, 250, 270, 288) sc.

Rnd 4: Rep Row 2 and mark bet sts 97 (107, 116, 125, 135, 144) and 98 (108, 117, 126, 136, 145) for "side seam" and carry marker upwards as you work.

Shape for Waist

Rnd 5 (dec rnd): Ch 1 and turn, sc in first sc, *sc2tog in next 2 sts, sc in each st across to within 3 sts of marker at "side seam," sc2tog in next 2 sts*, sc in each of next 2 sc, rep from * to * once, sc in last st—190 (210, 228, 246, 266, 284) sts.

Cont to alternate a rnd of dc with a rnd of sc and dec in patt every 3 rows 3 times more with 4 fewer sts after each dec rnd—178 (198, 216, 234, 254, 272) sts at end of last rnd. Work even on 178 (198, 216, 234, 254, 272) sts until piece measures 4½" (11.5 cm) total from beg or 21 rnds total.

Shape for Bust

Next Rnd (inc rnd): Maintaining est patt, work first st, *inc in next st, work even across to within 2 sts of marker at "side seam," inc in next st, work each of next 2 sts*; rep from * to * once, work even around to last st—182 (202, 220, 238, 258, 276) sts.

Cont to alternate a rnd of sc with a rnd of dc and inc in similar manner every 4 rows 6 times more with 4 more sts after each inc rnd.

Work even on 206 (226, 244, 262, 282, 300) sts until body measures 11" (28 cm) total from beg.

Back Armholes

Turn and sl st across first 5 (6, 8, 10, 12, 14) sts, maintaining established patt, work across next 93 (101, 106, 111, 117, 122) sts, do not work rem sts.

Maintaining established patt, dec 1 st at each end (one st in) on next row and every row 4 (6, 8, 8, 10, 12) times, then dec 1 st at each end (one st in) every other row 2 (3, 3, 4, 3, 2) times.

Work even in patt on 81 (83, 84, 87, 91, 94) sts until armholes measures 7 (7¼, 7½, 7¾, 8, 8¼)" (18 [18.5, 19, 19.5, 20.5, 21] cm) from beg of armhole shaping.

Shape Back Neck and Shoulders

Next Row: Turn and sl st across first 4 (4, 4, 4, 5, 5) sts, maintaining est patt, work in each of next 16 (16, 16, 17, 18, 19) sts, leaving center 41 (43, 44, 45, 45, 46) sts unworked, join another ball of yarn in next st, maintaining est patt, work in each of next 16 (16, 16, 17, 18, 19) sts,

leave rem sts unworked. Working both shoulders at same time, working sl sts at beginnings of rows and leaving sts unworked at ends of rows, bind off 4 (4, 4, 4, 5, 5) sts on shoulder edge and 2 sts on neck edge on next row; then bind off 4 (4, 4, 4, 4, 5) sts on shoulder edge and dec 1 st on neck edge on next row; then dec 1 sts on neck edge on next row—4 (4, 4, 5, 5, 5) sts rem.

Front Armholes

With appropriate side facing, sk 10 (12, 16, 20, 24, 28) sts to the left of first row of Back Armhole and join W in next st, work Front Armholes as for Back Armholes until armholes measure 4¾ (5, 5¼, 5½, 5¾, 6)" (12 [12.5, 13.5, 14, 14.5, 15] cm) from beg of armhole shaping.

Shape Front Neck

Maintaining established patt, work even across first 30 (30, 30, 31, 33, 34) sts, sk center 21 (23, 24, 25, 25, 26) sts, join another ball of yarn in next st and work across rem 30 (30, 30, 31, 33, 34) sts. Working both shoulders at same time, in same manner as on back, bind off 3 sts from each neck edge, then bind off 2 sts from each neck edge, then

dec 1 st from each neck edge on next row and every row 8 times, then dec 1 st from each neck edge every other row once. AT THE SAME TIME, when Front Armholes measure same as Back Armhole to shoulder shaping, shape shoulders same as back shoulders.

Finishing

Block piece to measurements. With W, sew shoulder seams.

Neck Trim

Rnd 1: With RS facing, join O in shoulder seam on neck edge, ch 1, sc evenly around neck opening, join with sl st to first sc.

Rnds 2 and 3: Ch 1, sc in each sc around, join with sl st to first sc. At end of last rnd, fasten and end off.

Armhole Trim

Starting at center bottom of armhole opening, rep Neck Trim around each armhole opening.

Bottom Trim

Starting at "side seam" on bottom edge, rep Neck Trim around bottom edge.

Not So Bling Jewelry

This subtle jewelry presents lots of options. Make pieces longer or shorter, make really short versions and add hooks for dangling earrings (instructions not included). Make several to coordinate with every outfit. The sheen of the yarn and the beads lend a certain dressiness without being gaudy, making them perfect for a variety of occasions and ensembles.

Finished Sizes

About 30½" (77.5 cm) long for Wine Spiral Necklace, 27¼" (69 cm) long for Olive Spiral Necklace, 19¼" (49 cm) for Beaded Necklace and 9½" (24 cm) for Beaded Bracelet. Make adjustments to lengths in beginning chains.

Materials

Yarn: Berroco/Lang Opal (58% nylon, 42% viscose, 50 g/about 168 yds [154 m]/50 g): #0099 olive (O) and #0063 wine (W), 1 skein each.
Crochet hook: Size C/2 (2.75 mm). Adjust hook size if necessary to obtain the correct gauge.
Beads: Glass seed beads, size 6, about 95 beads for bracelet and 190 beads for necklace (color 6-2035 Mt Met Khaki Iris, from Earth Bead Gallery.
Notions: Smooth, contrasting yarn as row marker.

Gauge

25 sc = 4" (10 cm).

Notes

Buttons and button loops are built in. Button is worked in the round with WS facing, do not join or turn, use contrasting yarn to mark beg/end of rnds.

Special Abbreviations

BUB (Bring up bead): [Snuggle the bead up close to the hook.] Beads lie on yarn strand behind sc.

Special Stitches

Bdc (Beaded double crochet): [Yarn around hook, pick up lp in next st], BUB, [yarn around hook and draw through 2 lps on hook] twice to complete st.

Wine Spiral Necklace

Button: With W, make a slipknot with the *tail* that closes up the slipknot. Always keep tail in the front of work, on WS.

Rnd 1: (WS) Ch 2, work 4 sc in 2nd ch from hook, do not join but mark beg/end of rows with contrasting piece of yarn, WS always faces—4 sc.

Rnd 2: Work 2 sc in each sc around—8 sc.

Rnd 3: Sc in each sc around—8 sc.

Rnd 4: Sl st in every other sc around to close—4 sl sts. Ch 190 for length of necklace, then ch 8 for button-loop, sl st to 8th ch from hook to close lp, ch 1 and work 12 sc into ch-8 button-lp, join with sl st to first sc—12 sc in lp.

Necklace: Ch 1, *work 3 sc in each of next 10 ch of necklace ch, work 3 dc in each of next 20 ch of necklace ch; rep from * across, ending with 3 sc in each of last 10 ch of necklace ch—570 sts. Fasten and end off, tie end tail to beg slipknot tail of button and hide inside button.

Olive Spiral Necklace

Button: With O, make a slipknot with the *tail* that closes up the slipknot. Always keep tail in the front of work, on WS.

Rnd 1: (WS) Ch 2, work 4 sc in 2nd ch from hook, do not join but mark beg/end of rows with contrasting piece of yarn, WS always faces—4 sc.

Rnd 2: Work 2 sc in each sc around—8 sc.

Rnd 3: Sc in each sc around—8 sc.

Rnd 4: Sl st in every other sc around to close—4 sl sts. Ch 170 for length of necklace, then ch 8 for button-loop, sl st to 8th ch from hook to close lp, ch 1 and work 12 sc into ch-8 button-lp, join with sl st to first sc—12 sc in lp.

Necklace: Ch 1, work 3 sc in each of next 35 ch of necklace ch, work 3 hdc in each of next 20 ch of necklace ch, work 3 dc in each of next 20 ch of necklace ch, work 3 trc in each of next 20 ch of necklace ch, work 3 dc in each of next 20 ch of necklace ch, work 3 hdc in each of next 20 ch of necklace ch, work 3 sc in each of next 35 ch of necklace ch—510 sts. Fasten and end off, tie end tail to beg slipknot tail of button and hide inside button.

Olive Beaded Necklace, Wine Beaded Bracelet

Pre-string appropriate number of beads onto yarn before working.

Button: With O (W), make a slip-knot with the *tail* that closes up the slipknot. Always keep tail in the front of work, on WS.

Rnd 1: (WS) Ch 2, work 4 sc in 2nd ch from hook, do not join but mark beg/end of rows with contrasting piece of yarn, WS always faces—4 sc.

Rnd 2: Work 2 sc in each sc around—8 sc.

Rnd 3: Sc in each sc around—8 sc.

Rnd 4: Sl st in every other sc to close—4 sl sts. Ch 120 (60) for length of necklace (bracelet), then ch 8 for button loop, sl st to 8th ch from hook to close lp, ch 1 and work 12 sc into ch-8 button-lp, join with sl st to first sc—12 sc in lp.

Necklace (Bracelet): Ch 1, *[dc, bdc, dc] in next ch of necklace (bracelet) ch, [bdc,dc, bdc] in next ch of necklace (bracelet) ch; rep from * across. Fasten and end off, tie end tail to beg slipknot tail of button and hide inside button.

Olive Spiral Necklace and Wine Spiral Necklace

Olive Beaded Necklace and Wine Beaded Bracelet

Full Metal Jacket

Dress up a classic with an etching of novelty-yarn trim. Add an interesting neckline and a yarn with pizzazz and go to town in this versatile piece. Wear it with jeans and lots of gold chains for a hip look, or dress it up with pumps and pearls.

Finished Size

36 (40, 44, 48, 52, 56)" (91.5 [101.5, 112, 122, 132, 142] cm) bust/chest circumference. This garment is intended to be loose-fitting. Sweater shown measures 40" (101.5 cm).

Materials

Yarn: Plymouth 24K (82% nylon, 18% lamé, 187 yd [171 m]/50 g): #1990 camouflage (A), 8 (9, 10, 11, 13, 14) skeins. Plymouth Flash (100% nylon, 190 yd [174 m]/50 g): #992 champagne (B), 1 (1, 2, 2, 2, 2) skeins.
Crochet hook: Size F/5 (3.75 mm) Adjust hook size if necessary to obtain correct gauge.
Notions: Six ⅞" buttons. Smooth contrasting yarn as marker.

Gauge

21 sts and 16 rows = 4" (10 cm) in hdc when steam blocked.

Notes

Body is worked in one piece up to the underarms. Sleeves are worked circularly in rnds up to the cap. Do not count ch-1s at beg of rows as a st.

Special Stitches

Hdc2tog (decrease one hdc): [Yarn around hook, pick up lp in next st] twice, yarn around hook and pull through rem lps on hook.
Sc2tog (decrease one single crochet): [Pick up lp in next st] twice, yarn around hook and pull through rem 3 lps on hook.
To "bind off" sts: At beg of row, sl st over stated number of sts, then sl st in next st to begin resuming work. At end of row, skip stated number of sts and do not work them.

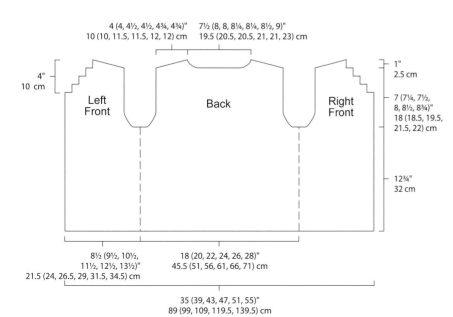

4 (4, 4½, 4½, 4¾, 4¾)"
10 (10, 11.5, 11.5, 12, 12) cm

7½ (8, 8, 8¼, 8¼, 8½, 9)"
19.5 (20.5, 20.5, 21, 21, 23) cm

4"
10 cm

Left Front   Back   Right Front

1"
2.5 cm

7 (7¼, 7½, 8, 8½, 8¾)"
18 (18.5, 19.5, 21.5, 22) cm

12¾"
32 cm

8½ (9½, 10½, 11½, 12½, 13½)"
21.5 (24, 26.5, 29, 31.5, 34.5) cm

18 (20, 22, 24, 26, 28)"
45.5 (51, 56, 61, 66, 71) cm

35 (39, 43, 47, 51, 55)"
89 (99, 109, 119.5, 139.5) cm

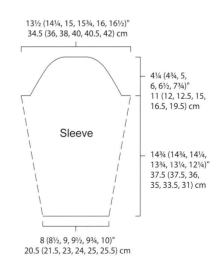

13½ (14¼, 15, 15¾, 16, 16½)"
34.5 (36, 38, 40, 40.5, 42) cm

Sleeve

4¼ (4¾, 5, 6, 6½, 7¾)"
11 (12, 12.5, 15, 16.5, 19.5) cm

14¾ (14¾, 14¼, 13¾, 13¼, 12¼)"
37.5 (37.5, 36, 35, 33.5, 31) cm

8 (8½, 9, 9½, 9¾, 10)"
20.5 (21.5, 23, 24, 25, 25.5) cm

Body

With A, loosely ch 185 (205, 225, 249, 269, 289).

Row 1 (WS): Hdc in 2nd ch from hook and in each ch across—185 (205, 225, 249, 269, 289) hdc.

Row 2 (RS): Ch 1 and turn (do not count ch-1 as a st), hdc in each st across.

Cont to work in hdc and mark bet st 45 (50, 55, 61, 66, 71) and st 46 (51, 56, 62, 67, 72) for one side "seam" bet sts 140 (155, 170, 188, 203, 218) and st 141 (156, 171, 189, 204, 219) for other side "seam."

Work until piece measures 12¾" (32 cm) from beg or 51 rows total.

Right Front Armhole

Row 1: With RS facing, work in hdc across first 42 (45, 48, 53, 57, 59) sts only, ending at armhole edge, turn.

Size S: Dec 1 hdc at armhole edge every other row 3 times total. Work even on 39 sts until armhole measures 4" (10 cm) total.

Size M: Dec 1 hdc at armhole edge every row twice, then every other row twice, then every 3rd row once. Work even on 40 sts until armhole measures 4¼" (11 cm) total.

Size L: Bind off 2 sts from armhole edge—46 sts, then dec 1 hdc at armhole edge every row twice, then every other row 3 times. Work even on 41 sts until armhole measures 4½" (11.5 cm) total.

Size XL: Bind off 2 sts from armhole edge twice—49 sts, then dec 1 hdc at armhole edge every row twice, then every other row 3 times, then every 3rd row once. Work even on 43 sts until armhole measures 5" (12.5 cm) total.

Size 2X: Bind off 2 sts from armhole edge 3 times—51 sts, then dec 1 hdc at armhole edge every row 3 times, then every other row 4 times. Work even on 44 sts until armhole measures 5½" (14 cm) total.

Size 3X: Bind off 3 sts from armhole edge, then bind off 2 sts from armhole edge twice—52 sts, then dec 1 hdc at armhole edge every row 5 times, then every other row twice. Work even on 45 sts until armhole measures 4¾" (12 cm) total.

Shape Stair-step Neck

From neck edge, bind off 5 sts on next row, then bind off 4 (5, 5, 5, 5, 5) st on next 4th row, then bind off 4 (4, 4, 5, 5, 5) sts on next 4th row, then bind off 4 (4, 4, 4, 4, 5) sts on next 4th row.

Shape Shoulder

AT THE SAME TIME, when armhole measures 7 (7¼, 7½, 8, 8½, 8¾)" (18 [18.5, 19, 20.5, 22] cm), bind off 5 sts from shoulder edge on next row; then bind off 4 (4, 4, 5, 5, 5) sts on next row; then bind off 4 (4, 4, 4, 5, 5) sts on next row; then bind off 4 (4, 5, 5, 5, 5) sts on next row—5 sts rem, fasten and end off.

Back Armhole

With RS facing, skip next 6 (10, 14, 16, 18, 24) sts past first row of Right Front Armhole and join A in next st, ch 1, hdc in same st as join and in next 88 (94, 100, 110, 118, 122) sts—89 (95, 101, 111, 119, 123) sts total.

Shape as for Right Front Armhole at both ends. Work even on 83 (85, 87, 91, 93, 95) sts until armholes measure 7 (7¼, 7½, 8, 8½, 8¾)" (18 [18.5, 19, 20.5, 22] cm).

Shape Back Neck and Shoulders

Bind off 5 sts from shoulder edge on next row; then bind off 4 (4, 4, 5, 5, 5) sts; then bind off 4 (4, 4, 4, 5, 5) sts on next row; then bind off 4 (4, 5, 5, 5, 5) sts on next row. AT THE SAME TIME, bind off center 31 (33, 33, 35, 35, 37) sts, work rem sts. Join a separate ball of yarn to other shoulder and work both shoulders at the same time and bind off 2 sts from each neck edge once, then dec 1 hdc at neck edge every row twice—5 sts rem on each shoulder. Fasten and end off.

Left Front Armhole

Row 1: With RS facing, skip next 6 (10, 14, 16, 18, 24) sts past first row of Back Armhole and join A in next st, ch 1, hdc in same st as join and in next 41 (44, 47, 52, 56, 58) sts—42 (45, 48, 53, 57, 59) sts.

Work the same as for Right Front, reversing shaping. Fasten and end off.

Sleeve (make 2)

With A, loosely ch 43 (45, 47, 49, 51, 53), join with sl st to first ch to form circle, being careful not to twist.

Rnd 1 (WS): Ch 1 (does not count as a st), hdc in each ch around—43 (45, 47, 49, 51, 53) hdc, join with sl st to first hdc.

Rnd 2: Ch 1 and turn, hdc in each hdc around, join with sl st to first hdc.

Rnd 3 (inc rnd): Ch 1 and turn, hdc in first hdc, 2 hdc in next hdc, hdc across to within last 2 hdc, 2 hdc in next hdc, hdc in last hdc—45 (47, 49, 51, 53, 55) sts, join with sl st to first hdc.

Cont working in hdc and rep inc rnd every other rnd 0 (0, 0, 0, 2, 6) times, then inc every 3rd rnd 4 (4, 10, 16, 14, 10) times, then inc every 4th rnd 10 (10, 5, 0, 0, 0) times.

Work even on 73 (75, 79, 83, 85, 87) sts until sleeves measure 14¾ (14¾, 14¼, 13¾, 13¼, 12¼)" (37.5 [37.5, 36, 35, 33.5, 31] cm) from beg.

Shape Cap

Work now progresses in rows.

Size S: Bind off 3 sts from each end on next row, (alternately bind off 2 sts from each end on next row, then dec 1 hdc on each end on next row) 8 times total, then dec from each end on next row— 17 sts, fasten and end off.

Size M: Bind off 5 sts from each end on next row, then dec 1 hdc from each end on next row and every row 14 times total, bind off 2 sts from each end on next row, then 3 sts from each end on next 3 rows—15 sts, fasten and end off.

Size L: Bind off 7 sts from each end on next row, then 2 sts from each end on next row, then dec 1 hdc from each end on next row and every row 17 times total, bind off 2 sts from each end on next row, then 4 sts from each end on next 2 rows—15 sts, fasten and end off.

Size XL: Bind off 8 sts from each end on next row, then 2 sts from each end on next 2 rows, then dec 1 hdc from each end on next row and every row 2 times total, then dec 1 hdc from each end every other row 3 times, then dec 1 st from each end on next row and every row 12 times total, bind off 2 sts from each end on next row—21 sts, fasten and end off.

Size 2X: Bind off 9 sts from each end on next row, then 2 sts from each end on next 2 rows, then dec 1 hdc from each end on next row and every other row 6 times total, then dec 1 hdc from each end every row 8 times, bind off 2 sts from each end on next 2 rows—19 sts, fasten and end off.

Size 3X: Bind off 7 sts from each end on next row, then 2 sts from each end on next 3 rows, then (alternately dec 1 hdc from each end on next 2 rows and every other row 1 time) 3 times total, then dec 1 hdc from each end every other row 4 times, then dec 1 hdc from each end every row 5 times, bind off 2 sts from each end on next 2 rows—17 sts, fasten and end off.

Finishing

Block pieces to measurements. Sew shoulder seams. Set in sleeves.

Bottom Trim

With RS facing and B, sc evenly across bottom edge, working into bottom of foundation ch. Work 2 rows even in sc, fasten and end off.

Button Band

With RS facing and B, work about 88 (89, 91, 93, 96, 97) sc evenly spaced along Left Front edge. Work 4 rows even in sc, then sl st in each st across, fasten and end off. Mark position for 6 buttons evenly spaced with top button 2 sts below neck edge and bottom button 1½" (3.8 cm) above bottom edge. Sew on buttons.

Buttonhole Band

With RS facing and B, work about 88 (89, 91, 93, 96, 97) sc evenly spaced along Right Front edge. Work another row of sc.

Buttonhole Row: For each corresponding button of Button Band, work ch 3 and skip 3 sc.

Next Row: Sc across and work 3 sc in each ch-3 buttonhole space.

Work another row of sc, then sl st in each st across, fasten and end off.

Neckband

With RS facing and B, sc evenly around neck edge, working 2 sc at outer corners and sc2tog at inner corners. Work another 2 rows in this manner, fasten and end off.

Faux Pockets (make 2)

With B, ch 23.

Row 1: Sc in 2nd ch from hook, sc in each ch across—22 sc.

Row 2: Ch 1 and turn, sc in each sc across, fasten and end off.

Sew one Pocket centered on each Front 4" (10 cm) above bottom edge. Weave in loose ends.

SEVEN

Circular Constructions

Before we get started, let me make a distinction between two types of circles in this chapter. There is crocheting in the round, which is actually a tube, and there's crocheting a circle. The former doesn't necessarily form a circle, but the latter does.

Working in the Round

A very common way to crochet is in the round. Working in the round certainly eliminates the need to seam. This entails joining the beginning of a row to the end with the use of a slip stitch, then turning the work to crochet a wrong-side row. Sometimes, when the stitch is short, as in a single crochet or a half double crochet, the work continues in a spiral and there is no joining at the end to the beginning of the round. There is no turning of the work and the right side always faces.

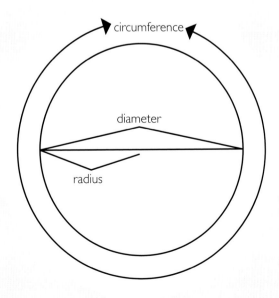

Working a Circle Shape

What determines the method depends on many factors. The look of the fabric changes when working in a continuous spiral. Since rows with the "wrong side" facing are not worked, the right side is smoother. The stitches are a bit skewed, however, as the stitches bias slightly to the right. When working in joined rounds back and forth, there is the "ridge" of the wrong-side row and a "jog" appears at the slip-stitch join, but the rows and stitches line up plumb.

Working a Circle Shape

The uses of a circle are many. They form yokes, hats, pouches, pillows, coasters, shawls, even some skirts. How does one figure out the stitches to be increased in order to form a flat disk? The answer lies in knowing your gauge (of course) and using the mathematical principles of pi. Fear not the math; it's not that bad.

There is a clear and proportional relationship between the widest part of a circle (known as diameter) and the distance around the outside of that circle (or circumference). That proportional relationship is pi, which is roughly equal to 3.14159 . . . (it's actually an infinite decimal that goes on forever, but 3.14 is sufficient).

So, if a circle measures 7 inches at its full width, it measures about 22 inches around the outside. This is perfect for the average human head, and therefore useful for a hat.

# of total rows	radius	diameter (2 x radius)	circumference around circle	# of stitches around to get circumference based on stitch gauge
	1"	2"	6.28"	
	2"	4"	12.56"	
	3"	6"	18.84"	
	4"	8"	25.12"	
	5"	10"	31.40"	
	6"	12"	37.68"	
	7"	14"	43.96"	
	8"	16"	50.24"	
	9"	18"	56.52"	
	10"	20"	62.8"	

Now, if we had a single-crochet gauge of 3 stitches and 4 rows = 1 inch, at row 14 (half the diameter, or radius), there should be 66 stitches around. What about the rows before that, though? I say set up a table.

The "radius" is the distance from the middle of the circle to the outside, or the total number of rows worked. Double this and you get the full width of the circle, or diameter. The number of inches in the circumference is fixed. Just multiply the row gauge by the radius for the number of rows, and then multiply the stitch gauge by the circumference to figure out how many stitches there should be on that row. Filling in the above table with our example, below, round the numbers of stitches to ones that will follow easier formulas of increases. On Row 4, use 18 stitches. On Row 8, use 36 stitches. On Row 12, make it 54 stitches. These are all multiples of 6. Then, on final row 14, it's easy to arrive at 66 stitches total. Break it down even further:

Row 1: Work 6 sc in a circle.
Row 2: Double the number—12 stitches.
Row 3: Increase in every other stitch—18 stitches.
Row 4: Work even.
Row 5: Increase in every 3rd stitch—24 stitches.
Row 6: Increase in every 4th stitch—30 stitches.
Row 7: Increase in every 5th stitch—36 stitches.
Row 8: Work even.
Row 9: Increase in every 6th stitch—42 stitches.
Row 10: Increase in every 7th stitch—48 stitches.
Row 11: Increase in every 8th stitch—54 stitches.
Row 12: Work even.
Row 13: Increase in every 9th stitch—60 stitches.
Row 14: Increase in every 10th stitch—66 stitches.
Remember, blocking is also key to obtaining a flat circle, even if the numbers are slightly off. Again, err on the side of smaller or too few stitches, rather than bigger or too many. You will find other ways of approaching a circle shape in the chevron hat and the shell stitch hat. Other examples of circularly working in the round are scattered throughout the book.

# of total rows	radius	diameter (2 x radius)	circumference around circle	# of stitches around to get circumference based on stitch gauge
4	1"	2"	6.28"	18.84
8	2"	4"	12.56"	37.68
12	3"	6"	18.84"	56.52

Accessories à la Russe

Feel like a czarina in this ensemble. The contrast of colors and textures come from the yarn, while the stitches are kept very simple. Note the neck shaping—the side-to-side neckband ensures a lower front neck so as not to choke the wearer. To see the stitches through the textured yarn, hold the work up to a light source (like a lamp).

Two-Toned Cape

Finished Size:
23" (58.5 cm) total length from base of collar, about 19" (48.5 cm) around neck, about 90" (228.5 cm) around bottom edge.

Materials
Yarn: Lily Chin Signature Collection Central Park (37% wool, 39% acrylic, 15% polyester, 7% viscose, 2% Lycra; 98 yds [90 m]/50 g): #3760 powder blue (A), 4 skeins. Lily Chin Signature Collection Tribeca (25% mohair, 43% wool, 17% viscose, 15% polyester: 153 yds [14 m]/50 g): #1276 midnight (B), 5 skeins.
Crochet hooks: Sizes K/10½ (6.5 mm) and J/10 (6 mm). Adjust hook size if necessary to obtain the correct gauge.
Notions: Two 1¼" (3.2 cm) buttons.

Gauge
With either A or B and larger hook, 10 hdc and 7 hdc rows = 4" (10 cm).
With B and smaller hook, 12 sc and 12 sc rows = 4" (10 cm).

Special Notes
- Collar is worked first from side to side, then sts are worked along bottom edge and rest of cape is worked from the top-down.
- Work off last 2 lps of old color with new color when changing colors. Basic stripe patt for body is 2 rows B, 2 rows A, 4 rows B, 2 rows A, 6 rows B, 2 rows A, 8 rows B, 2 rows A, 10 rows B, 2 rows A. Do not cut yarns but carry color not in use loosely along side edge except after Row 10 of body when rows of B exceed 6.

Special Stitches
Sc2tog (decrease one single crochet): [Pick up lp in next st] twice, yarn around hook and pull through rem 3 lps on hook.

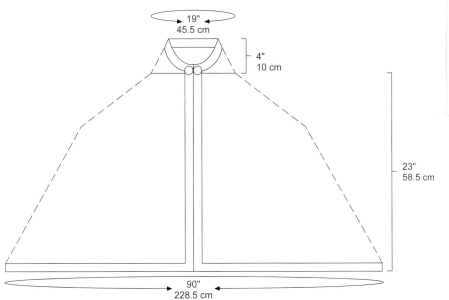

Neckband

With smaller hook and A, ch 3.

Row 1 (RS): Sc in 2nd ch from hook and next ch—2 sc.

Rows 2-4: Ch 1 and turn, sc in each st across—2 sc.

Row 5: Ch 1 and turn, 2 sc in first sc, sc in last sc—3 sc.

Rows 6 and 7: Ch 1 and turn, sc in each st across—3 sc.

Row 8: Ch 1 and turn, sc in each of first 2 sc, 2 sc in last sc—4 sc. Mark this end as top edge.

Working in sc throughout, inc at top edge on Rows 10, 11, 13, 14, 16, 17, 19, and 21.

Work even on 12 sts until collar measures about 12$\frac{1}{3}$" from beg or 37 rows total.

Cont to work in sc and dec 1 sc at top edge on rows 38, 40, 42, 43, 45, 46, 48, 49, 51, and 54.

Work even on 2 sts until collar measures about 19" (48.5 cm) from beg or 57 rows total, ending with RS row and changing to B at last st.

Body

Change to larger hook and with RS still facing, rotate piece to work across bottom edge of collar.

Row 1: With B, ch 1 (do not count ch 1 as st) work 48 hdc evenly spaced along bottom edge of collar—48 hdc.

Row 2: Ch 1 and turn (do not count ch 1 as st), hdc across and inc 12 sts evenly spaced across row, changing to A at last st—60 hdc.

Row 3: With A, ch 1 and turn (do not count ch 1 as st), hdc across and inc 12 sts evenly spaced across row—72 hdc.

Row 4: Ch 1 and turn, hdc across, changing to B at last st—72 hdc.

Row 5: With B, ch 1 and turn, hdc across and inc 12 sts evenly spaced across row—84 hdc.

Row 6: Ch 1 and turn, hdc across and inc 12 sts evenly spaced across row—96 hdc.

Row 7: Ch 1 and turn, hdc across and inc 12 sts evenly spaced across row—108 hdc.

Row 8: Ch 1 and turn, hdc across, changing to A at last st.

Row 9: With A, ch 1 and turn, hdc across and inc 12 sts evenly spaced across row—120 hdc.

Row 10: Ch 1 and turn, hdc across and inc 12 sts evenly spaced across row, changing to B at last st and ending off A. From here on, end off and rejoin A when necessary—132 hdc.

Row 11: With B, ch 1 and turn, hdc across and inc 12 sts evenly spaced across row—144 hdc.

Row 12: Ch 1 and turn, hdc across.

Row 13: Ch 1 and turn, hdc across and inc only 4 sts evenly spaced across row—148 hdc.

Row 14: Ch 1 and turn, hdc across and inc only 4 sts evenly spaced across row—152 hdc.

Row 15: Ch 1 and turn, hdc across and inc only 4 sts evenly spaced across row—156 hdc.

Rows 16-35: Rep Rows 12-15, working in the following color sequence: 1 more row B, 2 rows A, 8 rows B, 2 rows A, 7 rows B—216 hdc at end of last row.

Rows 36-38: Rep Rows 12-14—224 hdc at end of last row. Change to A at end of last row, end off B.

Row 39: With A, ch 1 and turn, hdc across.

Trim

With RS still facing, ch 1 for corner, rotate piece and sc evenly along Right Front Edge, ch 1 for corner, sc evenly across top of collar, ch 1 for corner, sc evenly along Left Front Edge, ch 1 for corner, join with sl st to beg hdc of Row 39.

Next Row: Ch 1 and turn, sc evenly around whole piece working 2 sc into ch-1 spaces of all corners, join with sl st to beg sc.

Next Row: Ch 1 and turn, sc evenly around whole piece, join with sl st to beg sc. Fasten and end off.

Finishing

Block piece to measurements. Sew buttons to each side of collar front. With A and smaller hook, crochet 12" chain and sew one end to base of Left Front button. Use this chain to close neck in "manila envelope/figure-eight" style.

Cossack Hat

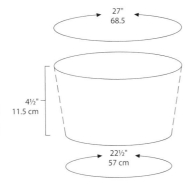

Finished Size

About 22½" (57 cm) around in circumference at head opening, 27" (68.5 cm) wide at widest point and 4½" (11.5 cm) deep.

Materials

Yarn: Lily Chin Signature Collection Central Park (37% wool, 39% acrylic, 15% polyester, 7% viscose, 2% Lycra; 98 yd [90 m]/50 g): #3760 powder blue, 2 skeins.

Crochet Hook: Size K/10½ (6.5 mm). Adjust hook size if necessary to obtain the correct gauge.

Notions: Smooth, contrasting yarn as row marker.

Gauge

8 sts = 3" (7.5 cm) in Slanted Pebble St (sc and dc in same st, see Rnds 13 and 14).

5 rows = 2" (5 cm) in sc in the round.

Notes

- Top of hat is worked in a spiral with RS facing, do not join or turn, use contrasting yarn to mark beg/end of rnds. Rest of hat is then worked back and forth and joined by sl st at end of rnds.

Special Stitches

Bpsc (Back-post single crochet): Insert hook from back-to-front-to-back around post of st, pick up lp, complete sc.

Slanted Pebble st: Sc and dc in same st (see Rnds 13 and 14).

Top

Rnd 1: Ch 2, work 8 sc in 2nd ch from hook, mark beg/end of rnd with contrasting piece of yarn, do not turn work.

Rnd 2: Work 2 sc in each sc around—16 sc.

Rnd 3: *Sc in next sc, 2 sc in next sc; rep from * around—24 sc.

Rnd 4: *Sc in each of next 2 sc, 2 sc in next sc; rep from * around—32 sc.

Rnd 5: *Sc in each of next 3 sc, 2 sc in next sc; rep from * around—40 sc.

Rnd 6: *Sc in each of next 4 sc, 2 sc in next sc; rep from * around—48 sc.

Rnd 7: Sc in each sc around—48 sc.

Rnd 8: *Sc in each of next 5 sc, 2 sc in next sc; rep from * around—56 sc.

Rnd 9: *Sc in each of next 6 sc, 2 sc in next sc; rep from * around—64 sc.

Rnd 10: *Sc in each of next 7 sc, 2 sc in next sc; rep from * around—72 sc.

Rnd 11: Dc in each sc around—72 dc.

Rnd 12: Bpsc in each dc around, join with sl st to first sc—72 bpsc.

Sides

Rnd 13: (WS) Ch 1 and turn, *[sc, dc] all in next sc, sk next sc; rep from * around, join with sl st to first sc—72 sts.

Rnd 14: Ch 1 and turn, * [sc, dc] all in next dc, sk next sc; rep from * around, join with sl st to first sc—72 sts.

Rnds 15–19: Rep Rnd 14.

Rnd 20: (RS) Ch 1 and turn, * work in patt for first 8 sts, sk next sc, sc in next dc, sk next sc, dc in next dc for double dec; rep from * around—60 sts.

Rnds 21 and 22: Rep Rnd 14, fasten and end off.

It's in the Bag

Two colorways and two types of paillettes lend different "purse-nalities" to these handbags. A unique construction allows this bag to be placed squarely flat on a surface without collapsing. A plastic-canvas lining enforces the bottom for structure. The use of raised front-post double-crochet stitches keeps corners permanently creased or folded.

Finished Size
Base = 8" (20 cm) × 4" (10 cm), Height = 6½" (16.5 cm).

Materials
Yarn: Trendsetter Sunshine (75% rayon, 25% nylon, 50 g/93 yd [85 m]/50 g): #51 grey (G) OR #03 champagne (C), 4 skeins per bag.
Crochet hook: Size D/3 (3.25mm). Adjust hook size if necessary to obtain the correct gauge.
Spangles/Paillettes: Trendsetter Chips (20 pieces per box): OZ120 Basil, Z89 Flambe, M72 Plum, M70 Dk. Wine, M69 Brown, 2 boxes each OR Sulyn Industries l.h. paillettes with large holes (75 pieces per package), ⁷⁄₈": silver, 200 total or 3 packages.
Notions: Plastic canvas (any gauge), cut to 8" (20 cm) × 4" (10 cm).

Gauge
22 sc and 25 sc rows = 4" (10 cm).

Special Notes
- Bottom rectangle is worked first for base of bag, then sts are worked around all edges for bag body.
- For multicolored version, randomly place spangles but use 4 of each color per ssc row.

Special Stitches
Ssc (Spangled single-crochet): With spangle in front, sc into spangle hole and next sc together.
Bpsc (Back-post single crochet): Insert hook from back-to-front-to-back around post of st, pick up lp, complete sc.
Fpdc (Front-post double crochet): Yarn around hook, insert hook from front-to-back-to-front around post of st, pick up lp, [yarn around hook and draw through 2 lps on hook] twice to complete st.

Base Rectangle

With either color throughout, loosely ch 44.
Base Row 1: Sc in 2nd ch from hook and in each ch across—43 sc.
Base Row 2: Ch 1 and turn, sc in each sc across—43 sc.
Rep Row 2 until piece measures 4" high or 25 rows total.

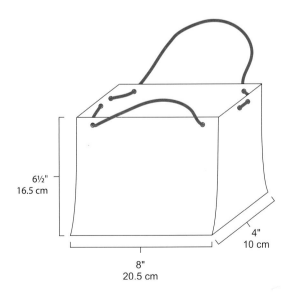

6½"
16.5 cm

4"
10 cm

8"
20.5 cm

Sides

Rnd 1: Ch 1 and turn, sc in each of 43 sc across, ch 1 for corner, with same side still facing, rotate piece and work 17 sc evenly spaced along side edge, ch 1 for corner, with same side still facing, rotate piece and working into bottom of beg foundation ch, sc in each of 43 ch, ch 1 for corner, with same side still facing, rotate piece and work 17 sc evenly spaced along other side edge, ch 1 for corner, join with sl st to first sc—120 sc plus 4 ch-1 corner spaces.

Rnd 2: Ch 2 and turn (does not count as a st), dc in each sc around and in each ch-1 space at corners, join with sl st to top of beg ch-2—124 dc.

Rnd 3 (RS): Ch 1 and turn, bpsc in each st around, join with sl st to first sc—124 bpsc.

Rnd 4 and all even rnds or WS rnds: Ch 1 and turn, sc in each st around, join with sl st to first sc.

Rnd 5: Ch 1 and turn, sc in each of next 25 sc across, fpdc around the post of next sc 2 rows below, sk the sc behind this fpdc, sc in each of next 17 sc, fpdc around the post of next sc 2 rows below, sk the sc behind this fpdc, sc in each of 25 ch, fpdc around the post of next sc 2 rows below, sk the sc behind this fpdc, sc in each of next 17 sc fpdc around the post of next sc 2 rows below, sk the sc behind this fpdc, join with sl st to first sc—124 sts including 4 fpdc at corners.

	sc
☒	ssc
ı	fpdc
	pattern repeat

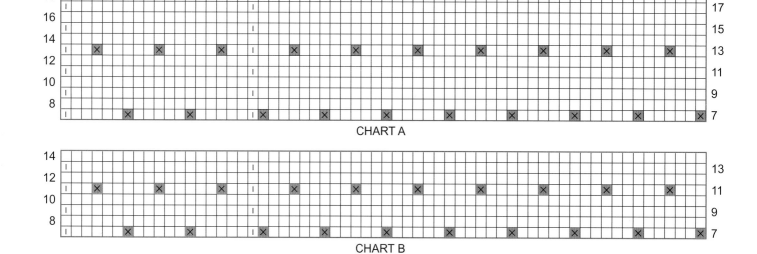

CHART A

CHART B

Rnd 6: Rep Rnd 4.

Rnds 7–40: Work following spangles chart A for multi-colored bag and chart B for gray bag. Read all odd-numbered (RS) rnds from right to left, then rep from right to left once; read all even-numbered rnds (WS) from left to right, then rep from left to right once.

For Chart A, rep Rnds 7–14; for Chart B, rep Rnds 7–18 until 40 rnds have been completed.

Rnd 41 (eyelet hole rnd): Ch 1 and turn, *sc in each of next 6 sc, ch 2 tightly, sk next sc, sc in each of next 27 sc, ch 2 tightly, sk next sc, sc in each of next 6 sc, fpdc around the post of next st 2 rows below, sk the sc behind this fpdc, sc in each of next 6 sc, ch 2 tightly, sk next sc, sc in each of next 3 sc, ch 2 tightly, sk next sc, sc in each of next 6 sc, fpdc around the post of next st 2 rows below, sk the sc behind this fpdc; rep from * once, join with sl st to first sc.

Rnd 42: Ch 1 and turn, sc in each sc and each ch-2 space around, join with sl st to first sc.

Rnds 43 and 44: Cont in patt, following appropriate chart for paillette placement.

Rnd 45: Turn and with RS facing, sl st in each st around, fasten and end off.

Strap

Make a ch 60–72" (152.5–183 cm) long, depending on preference, sc in 2nd ch from hook and in each ch across, turn. Sl st into each sc across, ch 1, with same side facing, rotate piece and working into bottom of beg foundation ch, sl st in each ch, fasten and end off leaving 4" (10 cm) tail.

Thread strap through eyelet holes of Rnd 41 as per schematic; using tail, sew ends of straps tog.

Sew plastic canvas to base inside bag.

Coming Full Circle Vest

Q: When is a circle not a circle? A: When it is a cocoon encompassing the wearer with a full shawl collar. Deceptively easy to crochet, the V-stitch lace increases evenly in a swirling pattern. Close with a pin or brooch, and you're good to go.

Finished Size

To fit 34 (38, 42, 46, 50, 54)" (86.5 [96.5, 106.5, 117, 127, 137] cm) bust/chest circumference. This garment is intended to be standard-fitting. Vest shown fits 34" (86.5 cm) bust.

Materials

Yarn: Lily Chin Signature Collection Chelsea (30% merino wool, 35% cotton, 35% acrylic, 191 yd [175 m]/50 g): #5811 power blue, 7 (8, 10, 11, 13, 14) skeins.
Crochet hook: size F/5 (3.75 mm). Adjust hook size if necessary to obtain the correct gauge.

Gauge

First 3 rnds = $3\frac{1}{2}$" (9 cm) in diameter; 6 V-sts (or 18 sts total) and 9 rows = 4" (10 cm) in V-st pattern.

Notes

Body is worked in one piece circularly in the round to the armholes. Arm slit openings are then added, yet piece is still worked circularly in the round.

Special Stitches

V-st: (Dc, ch 1, dc) all in same space.
V-st inc: (Dc, ch 1, dc, ch 1, dc) all in same space.
Picot: Ch 3, insert hook in front loop of last dc and in top-side loop of same last dc and work a sl st.

Body

Ch 4 and join with sl st in first ch.
Rnd 1 (RS): Ch 3 (counts as dc, ch 1), dc in ring to form first V-st, work 7 V-sts in ring, sl st in first ch-1 sp to join—8 V-sts.

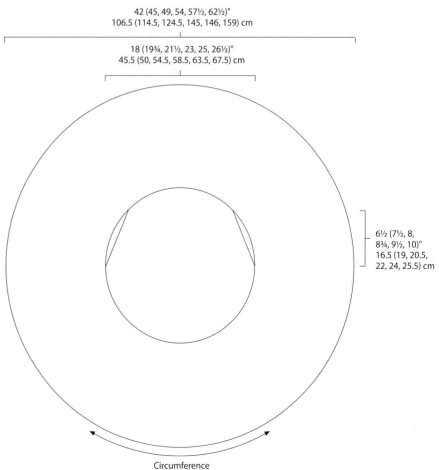

42 (45, 49, 54, 57½, 62½)"
106.5 (114.5, 124.5, 145, 146, 159) cm

18 (19¾, 21½, 23, 25, 26½)"
45.5 (50, 54.5, 58.5, 63.5, 67.5) cm

6½ (7½, 8, 8¾, 9½, 10)"
16.5 (19, 20.5, 22, 24, 25.5) cm

Circumference
132 (141½, 154, 169½, 180½, 196¼)"
335 (359.5, 391, 430.5, 458.5, 499) cm

STITCH KEY

- • = slip stitch (sl st)
- ⬭ = chain (ch)
- ⊤ = double crochet (dc)
- ⋁ = V-st
- ⋎ = V-st inc

Rnd 2: Ch 3 (counts as dc, ch 1), (dc, ch 1, dc) in same ch-1 sp as sl st, V-st inc in each ch-1 sp around, sl st in first ch-1 sp to join—16 ch-1 sps.

Rnd 3: Ch 3 (counts as dc, ch 1), dc in same ch-1 sp as sl st, V-st in each ch-1 space around, sl st in first ch-1 sp to join—16 V-sts.

Rnd 4: Ch 3 (counts as dc, ch 1), dc in same ch-1 sp as sl st, *V-st inc in next ch-1 sp, V-st in next ch-1 sp; rep from * around, ending with V-st inc in last ch-1 sp, sl st in first ch-1 sp to join—24 ch-1 sps.

Rnd 5: Ch 3 (counts as dc, ch 1), dc in same ch-1 sp as sl st, V-st in each ch-1 sp around, sl st in first ch-1 sp to join—24 V-sts.

Rnd 6: Ch 3 (counts as dc, ch 1), dc in same ch-1 sp as sl st, *V-st in next ch-1 sp, V-st inc in next ch-1 sp**, V-st in next ch-1 sp; rep from * around, ending last rep at **, sl st in first ch-1 sp to join—32 ch-1 sps.

Rnd 7: Ch 3 (counts as dc, ch 1), dc in same ch-1 sp as sl st, V-st in each ch-1 sp around, sl st in first ch-1 sp to join—32 V-sts.

Rnd 8: Ch 3 (counts as dc, ch 1), dc in same ch-1 sp as sl st, *V-st in each of next 2 ch-1 sps, V-st inc in next ch-1 sp**, V-st in next ch-1 sp; rep from * around, ending last rep at **, sl st in first ch-1 sp to join—48 ch-1 sps.

Rnd 9: Rep Rnd 7—48 V-sts.

Rnd 10: Ch 3 (counts as dc, ch 1), dc in same ch-1 sp as sl st, *V-st in each of next 3 ch-1 sps, V-st inc in next ch-1 sp**, V-st in next ch-1 sp; rep from * around, ending last rep at **, sl st in first ch-1 sp to join—56 ch-1 sps.

Rnd 11: Rep Rnd 7—56 V-sts.

Rnd 12: Ch 3 (counts as dc, ch 1), dc in same ch-1 sp as sl st, *V-st in each of next 4 ch-1 sps, V-st inc in next ch-1 sp**, V-st in next ch-1 sp; rep from * around, ending last rep at **, sl st in first ch-1 sp to join—64 ch-1 sps.

Rnd 13: Rep Rnd 7—64 V-sts.

Work in est patt until 21 (23, 25, 27, 29, 31) rnds total have been completed, working 8 V-st incs in each even-numbered rnd having one more V-st between incs—96

(104, 112, 120, 128, 136) V-sts at end of last rnd.
Piece should measure 18 (19³⁄₄, 21¹⁄₂, 23, 25, 26¹⁄₂)" (45.5
[50, 54.5, 58.5, 63.5, 67.5] cm) in diameter.

Open for Armholes

Rnd 22 (24, 26, 28, 30, 32): Ch 3 (counts as dc, ch 1),
    dc in same ch-1 sp as sl st, *V-st in each of next 9
    (10, 11, 12, 13, 14) ch-1 sps, V-st inc in next ch-1 sp,
    *ch 30 (33, 36, 39, 42, 45), skip next 10 (11, 12, 13,
    14, 15) ch-1 sps, V-st inc in next ch-1 sp*, (V-st in
    each of next 10 [11, 12, 13, 14, 15] ch-1 sps, V-st inc
    in next ch-1 sp] twice, rep from * to *, (V-st in each
    of next 10 [11, 12, 13, 14, 15] ch-1 sps, V-st inc in
    next ch-1 sp) 4 times, sl st in first ch-1 sp to join.
Rnd 23 (25, 27, 29, 31, 33): Ch 3 (counts as dc, ch 1),
    dc in same ch-1 sp as sl st, *V-st in each ch-1 sp to
    next armhole ch, (skip next ch, V-st in next ch, skip
    next ch) 10 (11, 12, 13, 14, 15) times*, rep from * to *
    once, V-st in each ch-1 sp around, sl st in first ch-1
    sp to join—96 (104, 112, 120, 128, 136) V-sts.
Work in established patt until 49 (53, 57, 63, 67, 73) rnds
total have been completed, working 8 V-st incs in each
even-numbered rnd, having one more V-st bet incs—200
(216, 232, 256, 272, 296) V-sts at end of last rnd.
Trim Rnd: Ch 1, sc in same ch-1 sp as sl st, *(3 dc,
    picot, 3 dc) in next ch-1 sp**, sc in next ch-1 sp; rep
    from * around, end last rep at **, sl st to first sc to
    join, fasten and end off.

Finishing
Block piece to measurements.

Armhole Trim
Join yarn at one end of one armhole slit, ch 3 (counts as
dc, ch 1), dc in same sp as sl st, work V-sts evenly spaced
around armhole opening, sl st in first ch-1 sp to join,
fasten and end off. Rep Armhole Trim around other
armhole opening.

EIGHT

Manipulating Lace

Lace projects are considered more advanced. Complex-looking stitchery belies a logical progression. Once the stitch pattern is mastered, manipulating it is half the fun.

Molly Ringwald Stole and Dress

I decided to play with tonal coordination for this duo rather than designing an exact match. Not only do these pieces incorporate tints and shades of a particular hue, yarn textures also vary. The same lace stitch from the stole is used in the skirt of the dress, however, for a more cohesive, complete look. Skirt shaping is done via changes to the size of the actual lace motif. If you are new to lace, try crocheting the stole first and familiarizing yourself with the stitch pattern before moving onto the dress.

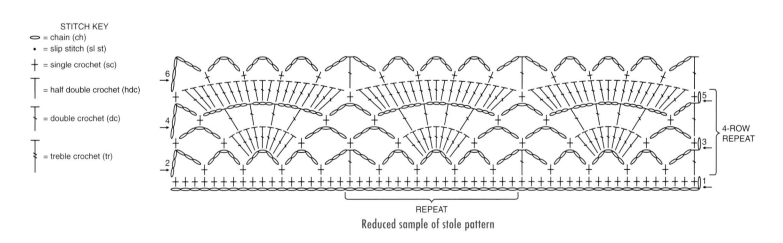

STITCH KEY
- ⬭ = chain (ch)
- • = slip stitch (sl st)
- + = single crochet (sc)
- T = half double crochet (hdc)
- = double crochet (dc)
- = treble crochet (tr)

REPEAT

4-ROW REPEAT

Reduced sample of stole pattern

Stole

Finished Size
18½" (47 cm) wide × 64" (162.5 cm) long.

Materials
Yarn: Karabella Lace Mohair (67% superkid mohair, 3% wool, 30% polyamid: 540 yd [494 m]/50 g): #3084 peachy-pink, 3 skeins.

Crochet hook: Size C/2 (2.75 mm). Adjust hook size if necessary to obtain the correct gauge.

Gauge
Three 18-st repeats (for total of 55 sts) = 8" (20.5 cm) and 12 rows = 4" (10 cm) in Lace stitch pattern.

Special Notes
- Stole begins at center. One half is completed towards the end, then the other half is picked up from foundation chain and also worked towards the end.

Lace Pattern
Ch a multiple of 18 plus 2 sts.

Row 1 (RS): Working in lps on back of ch sts, sc in 2nd ch from hook and in each ch across—multiple of 18 plus 1 st.

Row 2 (WS): Ch 6 and turn (counts as a dc and ch 3), sk first 3 sc, *sc in next sc, [ch 5, sk next 3 sc, sc in next sc] 3 times, ch 3, sk next 2 sc, dc in next sc**, ch 3, sk next 2 sc; rep from * across, ending last rep at **.

Row 3: Ch 1 and turn, sc in first dc, *ch 5, sc in next ch-5 lp, 9 dc in next ch-5 lp, sc in next ch-5 lp, ch 5, sc in next dc; rep from * across, ending with last sc in 3rd ch of beg ch-6 instead of into a dc.

Row 4: Ch 6 and turn (counts as a dc and ch-3), *sc in next ch-5 lp, [ch 3, sk next dc, dc in next dc] 4 times, ch 3, sc in next ch-5 lp**, ch 5; rep from * across, ending last rep at **, ch 3, dc in last sc.

Row 5: Ch 1 and turn, sc in first dc, sk next ch-3 lp and next sc, *[3 dc in next ch-3 lp, dc in next dc] 4 times, 3 dc in next ch-3 lp, sc in next ch-5 lp; rep from * across, ending with last sc in 3rd ch of beg ch-6 instead of into ch-5 lp.

Row 6: Ch 6 and turn (counts as a dc and ch-3), *sk next 3 dc, [sc in next dc, ch 5, sk next 3 dc] 3 times, sc in next dc, ch 3, sk next 3 dc, dc in next sc**, ch 3; rep from * across, ending last rep at **.

Rep Rows 3–6 for patt.

First Half
VERY loosely ch 128, begin Row 1 of Lace pattern—127 sc. Cont in Lace pattern until piece measures 32" (81.5 cm) from beg, ending with a row 5 of pattern, do not end off yarn.

Second Half
With WS facing, attach yarn to first ch on opposite side of foundation ch.

Working into bottom lps of beg foundation ch, begin with Row 2 of Lace pattern and work as for other half in same manner, do not end off.

Side Trims

With RS still facing, rotate work on its side and sc evenly spaced along side edge. Fasten and end off.
Go back to end of other half and with other yarn, rep along other side edge. Fasten and end off.

Dress

Finished Size

S (M, L, 1X, 2X, 3X): 33 (35¾, 37¾, 40½, 43¼, 45)" (84 [90.5, 96, 103, 110, 114.5] cm) bust/chest circumference. This is a close-fitting garment. Sample was done in size L.

Materials

Yarn: Lily Chin Signature Collection Chelsea (30% merino wool, 35% cotton, 35% acrylic, 191 yards [175 m]/50 g): #4917 salmon, 9 (9, 10, 11, 13, 14) skeins.
Crochet hook: Size F/5 (3.75 mm). Adjust hook size if necessary to obtain the correct gauge.
Notions: Smooth, contrasting colored yarn as markers.

Gauge

(*Note:* These are steamed and "hung" gauges.)
17 sts and 14 rows = 4" (10 cm) in Seed st pattern.
Small Fan Lace pattern = 2¼" (5.5 cm), 12 shell rows or three 4-row reps = 5½ (14 cm).
Medium Fan Lace pattern = 3½" (9 cm), 12 shell rows or three 4-row reps = 6" (15 cm).
Large Fan Lace pattern = 4¾" (12 cm), 12 shell rows or three 4-row reps = 6½" (16.5 cm).

Special Notes

• Bodice is worked in the round from the bottom up to the armholes, beg and ending at center back. Armholes are worked back and forth. Skirt is worked from the bottom of Bodice downwards. This is a seamless garment and may be tried on in progress.

Special Stitches

<u>Seed st (even number of sts):</u>

Rnd 1: Ch 1 [sc in next st, dc in next st] around, join with sl st in first sc.

Rnd 2 and all subsequent rows: Ch 1, [sc in dc, dc in sc] around, join with sl st in first sc.

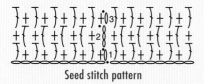

Seed stitch pattern

To work two consecutive inc's in Seed st pattern: Either [sc and dc] in each of 2 consecutive sts or [dc and sc] in each of 2 consecutive sts, according to pattern.

To "bind off" sts: At beg of row, slip st over stated number of sts, then sl st into next st to begin resuming work. At end of row, skip stated number of sts and do not work them.

Small Fan Lace pattern (worked in the round, multiple of 10 sts):

Rnd 1 (WS): Ch 5 and turn (counts as dc and ch 2), *[sk next sc, sc in next sc, ch 3] 3 times, sk next sc, sc in next sc, ch 2, sk next sc **, dc in next sc, ch 2; rep from * around, end last rep at **, sl st to 3rd ch of beg ch-5.

Rnd 2 (RS): Ch 1 and turn, sc in same ch as sl st, *ch 3, sc in next ch-3 lp, 5 dc in next ch-3 lp, sc in next ch-3 lp **, ch 3, sc in next dc; rep from * around, end last rep at **, ch 1, hdc into first sc.

Rnd 3: Ch 1 and turn, sc in first hdc, *[ch 3, sk next dc, dc in next dc] twice, ch 3, sc in next ch-3 lp **, ch 5, sc in next ch-3 lp; rep from * around, end last rep at **, ch 2, dc in first sc.

Rnd 4: Ch 1 and turn, sc in first dc, *[3 dc in next ch-3 lp, dc in

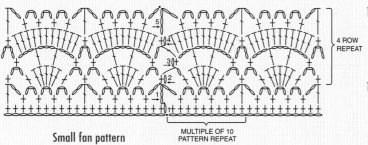

Small fan pattern

MULTIPLE OF 10 PATTERN REPEAT

4 ROW REPEAT

next dc] twice, 3 dc in next ch-3 lp **, sc in next ch-5 lp; rep from * across, end last rep at **, join with sl st to beg sc.

Rnd 5: Ch 5 and turn (counts as a dc and ch-2), *sk 2 dc, [sc in next dc, ch 3, sk next dc] 3 times, sc in next dc, ch 2, sk 2 dc **, dc in next sc, ch 2, sk 2 dc; rep from * across, end last rep at **, sl st to 3rd ch of beg ch-5.

Rep Rnds 2–5 for patt.

First Transition pattern, from Small to Medium Fan Lace (worked over one repeat):

Rnd 1 (WS): After any dc, ch 2, sk 2 dc, sc in next dc, ch 3, sk next dc, sc in next dc, ch 4, sk next dc, sc in next dc, ch 3, sk next dc, sc in next dc, ch 2, sk 2 dc, dc in next sc.

Rnd 2 (RS): After any sc in a dc, ch 4, sc in next ch-3 lp, 9 dc in next ch-4 lp, sc in next ch-3 lp, ch 4, sc in next dc.

Rnd 3: After sc in ch-4 lp before the 9 dc, [ch 3, sk next dc, dc in next dc] 4 times, ch 3, sc in next ch-4 lp.

Rnd 4: After sc in ch-5 lp, [3 dc in next ch-3 lp, dc in next dc] 4 times, 3 dc in next ch-3 lp, sc in next ch-5 lp.

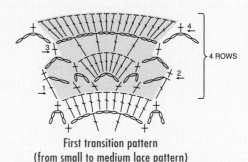

4 ROWS

First transition pattern
(from small to medium lace pattern)

Medium Fan Lace pattern (worked in the round):

Rnd 1 (WS): Ch 6 and turn (counts as a dc and ch-3), sk first 3 dc, *sc in next dc, [ch 5, sk next 3 dc, sc in next dc] 3 times, ch 3, sk 3 dc **, dc in next sc, ch 3, sk 3 dc; rep from * across, end last rep at **, join with sl st to 3rd ch of beg ch-6.

Rnd 2 (RS): Ch 1 and turn, sc in joining ch, *ch 5, sc in next ch-5 lp, 9 dc in next ch-5 lp, sc in next ch-5 lp **, ch 5, sc in next dc; rep from * across, end last rep at **, ch 2, dc in first sc.

Rnd 3: Ch 1 and turn, sc in first joining dc, *[ch 3, sk next dc, dc in next dc] 4 times, ch 3, sc in next ch-5 lp **, ch 5, sc in next ch-5 lp; rep from * across, end last rep at **, ch 2, dc in first sc.

Rnd 4: Ch 1 and turn, sc in first joining dc, *[3 dc in next ch-3 lp, dc in next dc] 4 times, 3 dc in next ch-3 lp **, sc in next ch-5 lp; rep from * across, end last rep at **, join with sl st to first sc.

Rep Rnds 1–4 for patt.

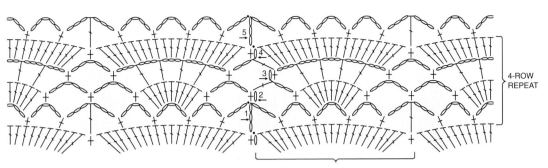

Medium fan pattern

Second Transition pattern, from Medium to Large Fan Lace (worked over one repeat):

Rnd 1 (WS): After any dc, ch 3, sk 3 dc, sc in next dc, ch 5, sk next 3 dc, sc in next dc, ch 6, sk next 3 dc, sc in next dc, ch 5, sk next 3 dc, sc in next dc, ch 3, sk 3 dc, dc in next sc.

Rnd 2 (RS): After any sc in a dc, ch 6, sc in next ch-5 lp, 13 dc in next ch-6 lp, sc in next ch-5 lp, ch 6, sc in next dc.

Rnd 3: After sc in ch-6 lp before the 13 dc, [ch 3, sk next dc, dc in next dc] 6 times, ch 3, sc in next ch-6 lp.

Rnd 4: After sc in ch-5 lp, [3 dc in next ch-3 lp, dc in next dc] 6 times, 3 dc in next ch-3 lp, sc in next ch-5 lp.

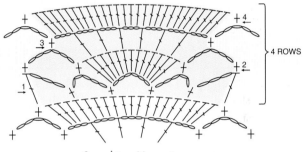

Second transition pattern
(from medium to large lace pattern)

Large Fan Lace pattern (worked in the round):

Rnd 1 (WS): Ch 7 and turn (counts as a dc and ch-4), sk first 4 dc, *sc in next dc, [ch 7, sk next 5 dc, sc in next dc] 3 times, ch 4, sk 4 dc **, dc in next sc, ch 4, sk 4 dc; rep from * across, end last rep at **, join with sl st to 3rd ch of beg ch-7.

Rnd 2 (RS): Ch 1 and turn, sc in joining ch, *ch 7, sc in next ch-7 lp, 13 dc in next ch-5 lp, sc in next ch-5 lp **, ch 7, sc in next dc; rep from * across, end last rep at +, ch 3, trc in first sc.

Rnd 3: Ch 1 and turn, sc in first joining trc, *[ch 3, sk next dc, dc in next dc] 6 times, ch 3, sc in next ch-7 lp **, ch 7, sc in

next ch-7 lp; rep from * across, end last rep at **, ch 3, trc in first sc.

Rnd 4: Ch 1 and turn, sc in first joining trc, *[3 dc in next ch-3 lp, dc in next dc] 6 times, 3 dc in next ch-3 lp **, sc in next ch-7 lp; rep from * across, end last rep at **, join with sl st to first sc.

Rep Rnds 1–4 for patt.

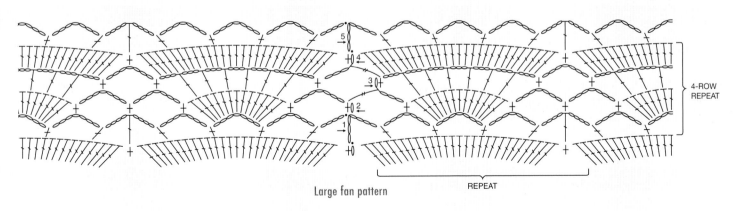

Large fan pattern   REPEAT

Bodice

Loosely ch 108 (120, 128, 140, 152, 160). Join with sl st to beg of ch, being careful not to twist. Begin Seed st as follows:

Rnd 1 (WS): Ch 1, sc in same ch as join, dc in next ch, *sc in next ch, dc in next ch; rep from * across, join with sl st to first sc.

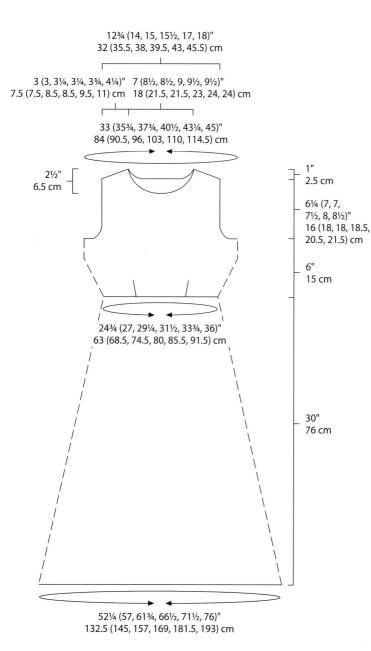

12¾ (14, 15, 15½, 17, 18)"
32 (35.5, 38, 39.5, 43, 45.5) cm

3 (3, 3¼, 3¼, 3¾, 4¼)" 7 (8½, 8½, 9, 9½, 9½)"
7.5 (7.5, 8.5, 8.5, 9.5, 11) cm 18 (21.5, 21.5, 23, 24, 24) cm

33 (35¾, 37¾, 40½, 43¼, 45)"
84 (90.5, 96, 103, 110, 114.5) cm

2½"
6.5 cm

1"
2.5 cm

6¼ (7, 7, 7½, 8, 8½)"
16 (18, 18, 18.5, 20.5, 21.5) cm

6"
15 cm

24¾ (27, 29¼, 31½, 33¾, 36)"
63 (68.5, 74.5, 80, 85.5, 91.5) cm

30"
76 cm

52¼ (57, 61¾, 66½, 71½, 76)"
132.5 (145, 157, 169, 181.5, 193) cm

Rnd 2 (RS): Ch 1 and turn, sc in first dc, dc in next sc, *sc in next dc, dc in next sc; rep from * across and place contrasting yarn markers between sts 11 and 12 (12 and 13, 12 and 13, 13 and 14, 14 and 15, 14 and 15) for first Back Dart, between sts 27 and 28 (30 and 31, 32 and 33, 35 and 36, 38 and 39, 40 and 41) for first Side Dart, between sts 39 and 40 (44 and 45, 48 and 49, 53 and 54, 58 and 59, 62 and 63) for first Front Dart, between sts 69 and 70 (76 and 77, 80 and 81, 87 and 88, 94 and 95, 98 and 99) for second Front Dart, between sts 81 and 82 (90 and 91, 96 and 97, 105 and 106, 114 and 115, 120 and 121) for second Side Dart, and between sts 97 and 98 (108 and 109, 116 and 117, 127 and 128, 138 and 139, 146 and 147) for second Back Dart, join with sl st to first sc, carry all markers upwards from here on.

Rnd 3 (WS, inc rnd): Ch 1 and turn, sc in first dc, dc in next sc, *sc in next dc, dc in next sc; rep from * around and inc 2 sts in pattern before and after each of the Front and Back Dart markers (there are 4 total), join with sl st to first sc—116 (128, 136, 148, 160, 168) sts.

Rnd 4 (RS, inc rnd): Work in Seed St pattern and inc before and after each of the Side Dart markers (there are 2 total), join with sl st to first sc—120 (132, 140, 152, 164, 172) sts.

Rnd 5: Work even in Seed St pattern.

Rnd 6 (inc rnd): Rep Rnd 3—128 (140, 148, 160, 172, 180) sts.

Rnd 7: Work even in Seed St pattern.

Rnd 8 (inc rnd): Rep Rnd 4—132 (144, 152, 164, 176, 184) sts.

Work in Seed St pattern and rep Rnd 4 every 4th rnd twice more with 4 more sts in each inc rnd—140 (152, 160, 172, 184, 192) sts.

Work even in Seed St pattern until piece measures 6" (15 cm), end ready to work a RS row, fasten and end off.

Shape Back Armholes

With RS facing, sk first 4 (4, 4, 6, 6, 6) sts of Back from right-side marker, join yarn to next st, ch 1 and sc in same st, work across rem 61 (67, 71, 73, 79, 83) sts in Seed St pattern—62 (68, 72, 74, 80, 84) sts.

Keeping to Seed St pattern, dec 1 st from each armhole edge on next 4 rows—54 (60, 64, 66, 72, 76) sts.

Work even in Seed St pattern until armholes measure 6¼ (7, 7, 7½, 8, 8½)" (16 [18, 18, 18.5, 20.5, 21.5] cm), end ready to work a RS row.

Shape Back Neck and Shoulders

Keeping to patt, bind off 2 (2, 3, 3, 4, 4) sts at each end of next row, then 3 sts at each end of foll row, then 2 (2, 2, 2, 3, 4) sts at each end of foll row, then 3 sts at each end of foll row. AT THE SAME TIME, leave center 26 (32, 32, 34, 36, 36) sts unworked, join separate ball of yarn to other shoulder and work both shoulders at the same time, dec from each neck edge 1 st over the next 2 rows, work even—2 (2, 3, 3, 3, 4) sts remain in each shoulder. Fasten and end off.

Shape Front Armholes

With RS facing, sk 8 (8, 8, 12, 12, 12) sts past last st of row 1 for Back Armhole, join yarn to next st and work as for Back Armhole until armholes measure 4¾ (5½, 5½, 6, 6½, 7)" (12 [14, 14, 15, 16.5, 18] cm).

Shape Front Neck

Keeping to patt, on next row, leave center 14 (20, 20, 22, 24, 24) sts unworked, join separate ball of yarn to other shoulder and work both shoulders at the same time, dec from each neck edge 1 st over the next 8 rows, work even.

Shape Front Shoulders

AT THE SAME TIME, when Front armholes measure same as Back to shoulders, shape for shoulders as for Back—2 (2, 3, 3, 3, 4) sts remain. Fasten and end off.

Skirt

With RS facing, join to center back, ch 1 and sc 110 (120, 130, 140, 150, 160) sts evenly around bottom of Bodice (sizes S and L will inc 2 sts evenly and size 2X will dec 2 sts evenly), join with sl st to first sc.

Rnds 1–4: Work Small Fan Lace pattern Rnds 1–4, working 11 (12, 13, 14, 15, 16) pattern repeats around skirt.

Rnds 5–8: *Work First Transitional pattern Rnds 1–4 for first repeat, then continue with Small Fan Lace pattern Rnd 5 and then Rnds 2–4 for next repeat; rep from *—that is, Alternate First Transitional pattern with Small Fan Lace pattern. (*Note:* Sizes S, L, and 2X will have First Transitional pattern at beg and end of rnds due to odd number of repeats.)

Rnds 9–12: *Work Medium Fan Lace pattern Rnds 1–4 for first repeat, then continue with Small Fan Lace pattern Rnd 5 and then Rnds 2–4 for next repeat; rep from *—that is, Alternate Medium Fan Lace pattern with Small Fan Lace pattern. (*Note:* Sizes S, L, and 2X will have Medium Fan Lace pattern at beg and end due to odd number of repeats.)

Rnds 13–16: *Continue with Medium Fan Lace pattern Rnds 1–4 for first repeat, then work First Transitional pattern Rnds 1–4 for next repeat; rep from *—that is, Alternate Medium Fan Lace pattern with First Transitional pattern. (*Note:* Sizes S, L, and 2X will have Medium Fan Lace pattern at beg and end of rnds due to odd number of repeats.)

Rnds 17–24: Work 8 rnds of Medium Fan Lace pattern—that is, work Rnds 1–4 twice.

Rnds 25–28: *Work Second Transitional Pattern Rnds 1–4 for first repeat, then continue with Medium Fan Lace pattern Rnds 1–4 for next repeat; rep from *—that is, Alternate Second Transitional pattern with Medium Fan Lace pattern. (*Note:* Sizes S, L, and 2X will have Second Transitional pattern at beg and end of rnds due to odd number of repeats.)

Rnds 29–32: *Work Large Fan Lace pattern Rnds 1–4 for first repeat, then continue with Medium Fan Lace pattern Rnds 1–4 for next repeat; rep from *—that is, Alternate Large Fan Lace pattern with Medium Fan Lace pattern. (*Note:* Sizes S, L, and 2X will have Large Fan Lace pattern at beg and end of rnds due to odd number of repeats.)

Rnds 33–40: Work 8 more rnds of this configuration—that is, work Rnds 1–4 twice.

Rnds 41–44: *Continue with Large Fan Lace pattern Rnds 1–4 for first repeat, then begin Second Transitional pattern Rnds 1–4 for next repeat; rep from *—that is, Alternate Large Fan Lace pattern with Second Transitional pattern. (*Note:* Sizes S, L, and 2X will have Large Fan Lace pattern at beg and end of rnds due to odd number of repeats.)

Rnds 45–60: Work 16 rnds of Large Fan Lace pattern—that is, work Rnds 1–4 four times.

Fasten and end off.

Finishing

Block piece to measurements. Sew shoulder seams. Work 2 rnds of sc evenly around neck and armhole edges.

The Lady Who Lunches Sheath and Gloves

Interior darts shape this retro-inspired dress. Matching fingerless gloves update the look while keeping it feminine. Wear a slip dress underneath the sheath for modesty or layer the dress over a T-shirt and leggings for a sportier, fashion-forward take.

Sheath

Finished Sizes

36½ (38½, 40½, 42½)" (92.5 [98, 103, 108] cm) bust/chest circumference. This is a standard-fitting garment. Sweater shown measures 38½" (98 cm).

Materials

Yarn: Lily Chin Signature Collection Chelsea (30% merino wool, 35% cotton, 35% acrylic, 191 yd [175 m]/1¾ oz [50 g]): #5825 stone, 7 (7, 8, 9) skeins.

Crochet hook: Size E/4 (3.5 mm) (F/5 [3.75 mm], G/6 [4 mm], H/8 [5 mm]). Adjust hook size if necessary to obtain the correct gauge. Note that hook size determines size of garment.

Notions: Smooth, contrasting colored yarn as markers or coilless safety pins. Yarn needle.

Gauge

(*Note:* These are steamed and "hung" gauges.)

For size 36½", 3 reps (or 24 sts total) = 5" (12.5 cm) and 13 patt rows = 6" (15 cm) on size E hook.

For size 38½", 4 reps (or 32 sts total) = 7" (18 cm) and 11 patt rows = 6" (15 cm) on size F hook.

For size 40½", 3 reps (or 24 sts total) = 5½" (14 cm) and 10 patt rows = 6" (15 cm) on size G hook.

For size 42½", 4 reps (or 32 sts total) = 7¾" (19.5 cm) and 8 patt rows = 6" (15 cm) on size H hook.

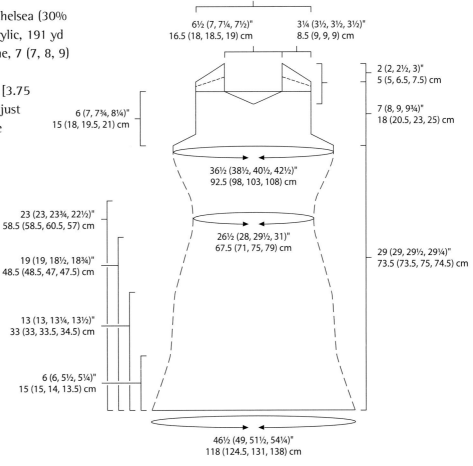

13 (14, 14½, 15½)"
33 (35.5, 37, 39.5) cm

6½ (7, 7¼, 7½)"
16.5 (18, 18.5, 19) cm

3¼ (3½, 3½, 3½)"
8.5 (9, 9, 9) cm

2 (2, 2½, 3)"
5 (5, 6.5, 7.5) cm

7 (8, 9, 9¾)"
18 (20.5, 23, 25) cm

6 (7, 7¾, 8¼)"
15 (18, 19.5, 21) cm

36½ (38½, 40½, 42½)"
92.5 (98, 103, 108) cm

23 (23, 23¾, 22½)"
58.5 (58.5, 60.5, 57) cm

26½ (28, 29½, 31)"
67.5 (71, 75, 79) cm

19 (19, 18½, 18¾)"
48.5 (48.5, 47, 47.5) cm

29 (29, 29½, 29¼)"
73.5 (73.5, 75, 74.5) cm

13 (13, 13¼, 13½)"
33 (33, 33.5, 34.5) cm

6 (6, 5½, 5¼)"
15 (15, 14, 13.5) cm

46½ (49, 51½, 54¼)"
118 (124.5, 131, 138) cm

Notes

- Body is worked in one piece circularly in the round to the armholes, beg and ending at center back. Armholes are worked back and forth. Shoulder shaping occurs only in front shoulder pieces.

Special Stitches

V-st: (Dc, ch 1, dc) all in same st.

Shell St: 5 dc all in same ch-1 space.

Either V-st or Shell st will be referred to as units.

5-Row Increase Sequence (see diagram):

Row 1: Work up to designated V-st, work 7-dc shell instead of 5-dc in next V-st.

Row 2: Work up to 7-dc shell, skip first of these 7 dc, dc in 2nd dc, ch 1, dc in 4th dc, ch 1, dc in 6th dc, skip last of these 7 dc.

Row 3: Work up to dc's above 7-dc shell, 3-dc shell in first dc, dc in next dc, 3-dc shell in last dc.

Row 4: Work up to first 3-dc shell of previous row, V-st in 2nd dc of next 3-dc shell, skip next dc of 3-dc shell, 3-dc shell in next dc, V-st in 2nd dc of next 3-dc shell.

Row 5: Work up to 3-dc shell of previous row, V-st in 2nd dc of this 3-dc shell.

4-Row Decrease Sequence (see diagram):

Row 1: Work up to designated V-st, work 3-dc shell instead of 5-dc in next V-st.

Row 2: Work up to V-st before 3-dc shell of previous row but work 3-dc shell instead of 5-dc in next V-st, V-st in 2nd dc of 3-dc shell, work 3-dc shell instead of 5-dc in next V-st.

Row 3: Work up to first 3-dc shell of previous row, dc in 2nd dc of 3-dc shell, dc in next V-st, dc in 2nd dc of next 3-dc shell.

Row 4: Work up to 3 dc of dec, work 5-dc shell in 2nd of these 3 dc.

STITCH KEY

⬭ = chain (ch)

• = slip stitch (sl st)

┬ = double crochet (dc)

= V-st (dc, ch 1, dc)

= Shell st (5 dc)

= 3-dc shell st

= 7-dc shell st

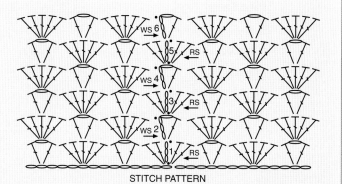

STITCH PATTERN

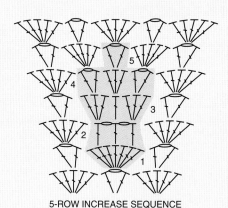

5-ROW INCREASE SEQUENCE

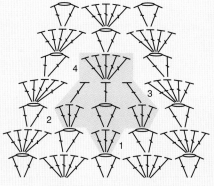

4-ROW DECREASE SEQUENCE

Body

With designated hook for desired size, very loosely ch 224, join with sl st to first ch to form circle being careful not to twist.

Rnd 1 (RS): Ch 3 (counts as dc), work 2 more dc in same ch as sl st, *skip next 3 ch, V-st (or dc, ch 1, dc) into next ch, skip next 3 ch**, Shell st (or 5 dc) in next ch; rep from * around, ending last rep at **, work 2 more dc into same ch as joining sl st, join with sl st to top of beg ch-3, you are at center Back and there are 56 units or 28 patt reps total.

Rnd 2 (WS): Ch 4 (counts as dc, ch 1) and turn, dc in same dc as sl st, *Shell st in ch-1 sp of next V-st**, V-st in 3rd dc of next Shell st; rep from * around, ending last rep at **, join with sl st in 3rd ch of beg ch-4.

Rnd 3 (RS): Sl st into next ch-1 sp, turn, ch 3 (counts as dc), work 2 more dc in same ch-1 sp as sl st, *V-st in 3rd dc of next Shell st**, Shell st in ch-1 sp of next V-st; rep from * around, end last rep at **, work 2 more dc into same ch-1 sp as beg sl st, join with sl st to top of beg ch-3.

Rep Rows 2 and 3 for patt throughout.

Rnd 4: Ch 4 (counts as dc, ch 1) and turn, dc in same dc as sl st, work as for Rnd 2 and after working 4 more units past beg ch-4 and dc, work next unit and mark for dart line, work another 8 more units, work next unit and mark for side line, work another 8 more units, work next unit and mark for dart line, work another 9 more units, work next unit and mark for dart line, work another 8 more units, work next unit and mark for side line, work another 8 more units, work next unit and mark for dart line, work last 4 units, join with sl st in 3rd ch of beg ch-4. Carry markers up as work progresses.

Work even in est patt (Shell sts over V-sts and V-sts over Shell sts) until 13 (11, 9, 7) rows total have been worked or until work measures 6 (6, 5½, 5¼)" (15 [15, 14, 13.5] cm), ending with a V-st at each of the 4 dart lines.

First Dec Sequence

Beg 4-row dec sequence at each of the 4 dart lines—48 units or 24 patt reps rem at end of 4 rows.

Work even in est patt until 28 (24, 22, 18) rows total have been worked or until work measures 13 (13, 13$\frac{1}{4}$, 13$\frac{1}{2}$)" (33 [33, 33.5, 34.5] cm), ending with a V-st at each of 2 side lines.

Second Dec Sequence

Beg 4-row dec sequence at each of the 2 side lines—44 units or 22 patt reps rem at end of 4 rows.

Work even in est patt until 41 (35, 31, 25) rows total have been worked or until work measures 19 (19, 18$\frac{1}{2}$, 18$\frac{3}{4}$)" (48.5 [48.5, 47, 47.5] cm), ending with a V-st at each of the 2 side lines, and a Shell st at each of the 4 dart lines.

Third and Fourth Dec Sequences

Beg 4-row dec sequence at each of the 2 side lines on next row, then beg 4-row dec sequence at each of the 4 dart lines on the row after that—32 units or 16 patt reps rem after all decreases have been completed.

Work even in est patt until 50 (42, 38, 30) rows total have been worked or until work measures 23 (23, 23$\frac{3}{4}$, 22$\frac{1}{2}$)" (58.5 [58.5, 63, 57] cm), ending with a V-st at each of the 2 side lines and a Shell st at each of the 4 dart lines.

First and Second Inc Sequences

Beg 5-row inc sequence at each of the 2 side lines on next row, then beg 5-row inc sequence at each of the 4 dart lines on the row after that—44 units or 22 patt reps rem at the end of all increases.

Work even in est patt until 63 (53, 49, 39) rows total have been worked or until work measures 29 (29, 29$\frac{1}{2}$, 29$\frac{1}{4}$)" (73.5 [73.5, 75, 74.5] cm), ending with a V-st at each of the 2 side lines, fasten and end off.

Back Armholes

Row 1 (RS): With RS of Back facing, skip V-st at right-hand side line marker, join yarn in 3rd dc of next Shell st, ch 3 (counts as dc), *Shell st in next V-st, V-st in next Shell st; rep from * across until 19 units total have been worked (do not count beg dc), dc in 3rd dc of next Shell st.

Row 2 (WS): Turn, sl st up to and including 3rd dc of first Shell, ch 3 (counts as dc), *Shell st in next V-st, V-st in next Shell st; rep from * across until 17 units total have been worked (do not count beg dc), dc in 3rd dc of last Shell st.

Row 3: Rep Row 2—15 units total with dc at beg and end.

Row 4: Ch 3 (counts as dc) and turn, *V-st in next Shell St**, Shell St in next V-st; rep from *, end last rep at **, dc in last dc.

Row 5: Ch 3 (counts as dc) and turn, *Shell St in next V-st**, V-st in next Shell St; rep from *, end last rep at **, dc in top of ch-3.

Row 6: Ch 3 (counts as dc) and turn, *V-st in next Shell St**, Shell St in next V-st; rep from *, end last rep at **, dc in top of ch-3.

Rep Rows 5 and 6 until 13 (13, 13, 11) Armhole rows total have been worked or until armholes measure 6 (7, 7$\frac{3}{4}$, 8$\frac{1}{4}$)" (15 [18, 19.5, 21] cm), fasten and end off.

Front Armholes

Work as for Back Armholes until 9 (9, 9, 7) rows total have been worked or until armholes measure 4 (5, 5$\frac{1}{2}$, 5$\frac{1}{4}$)" (10 [12.5, 14, 13.5] cm) and dead-center unit is a V-st.

Shape Right Front

Next Row (WS): Ch 3 (counts as dc) and turn, *V-st in next Shell st**, Shell St in next V-st; rep from * until 6 units total have been worked (do not count beg dc), dc in 3rd dc of next Shell St.

Next Row (RS): Turn, sl st up to and including 3rd dc of first Shell, ch 3 (counts as dc), *Shell St in next V-st, V-st in next Shell St; rep from * across until 5 units total have been worked (do not count beg dc), dc in top of ch-3.

Next Row: Ch 3 (counts as dc) and turn, (V-st in next Shell St, Shell St in next V-st) twice, dc in 3rd dc of next Shell St.

Next Row: Ch 3 (counts as dc) and turn, (V-st in next Shell St, Shell St in next V-st) twice, dc in top of beg ch-3.

Next Row: Ch 3 (counts as dc) and turn, (Shell St in next V-st, V-st in next Shell St) twice, dc in top of beg ch-3.

Next Row: Ch 3 (counts as dc) and turn, (V-st in next Shell St, Shell St in next V-st) twice, dc in top of beg ch-3.

Shape Right Shoulder

Next Row (WS): Ch 3 (counts as dc) and turn, Shell St in next V-st, V-st in next Shell St, Shell St in next V-st, dc in 3rd dc of next Shell St.

Next Row (RS): Turn, sl st up to and including 3rd dc of first Shell, ch 3 (counts as dc), Shell St in next V-st, V-st in next Shell St, dc in top of beg ch-3.

Next Row (WS): Ch 3 (counts as dc) and turn, Shell St in next V-st, dc in 3rd dc of next Shell St.

Last Row (RS): Turn, sl st up to and including 3rd dc of first Shell, ch 3 (counts as dc), dc in top of beg ch-3, fasten and end off.

Shape Left Front

Next Row: With WS facing, skip dead-center V-st, join yarn in 3rd dc of next Shell St, ch 3 (counts as dc), (Shell St in next V-st, V-st in next Shell St) 3 times, dc in top of beg ch-3.

Cont to work as for Right Front reversing all shaping.

Finishing

Block piece to measurements. Sew Front shoulder seams to straight section of Back.

Neck Trim

Rnd 1: With WS facing, join yarn at one shoulder seam, ch 1, sc evenly around neck edge, join with sl st to beg sc.

Rnd 2: Turn, ch 1, sc in each sc around, join with sl st to beg sc, fasten and end off.

Armhole Trim

With WS facing, join yarn at underarm, rep Neck Trim around armhole. Rep Armhole Trim around other armhole.

Gloves

Finished Sizes

Women's glove size 5 (6, 7, 8). Sample is worked in size 6.

Materials

Yarn: Lily Chin Signature Collection Chelsea (30% merino wool, 35% cotton, 35% acrylic, 191 yd [175 m]/1¾ oz [50 g]): #5825 stone, 2 skeins.

Crochet hook: Size E/4 (3.5 mm) (F/5 [3.75 mm], G/6 [4 mm], H/8 [5 mm]). Adjust hook size if necessary to obtain the correct gauge. Note that hook size determines size of gloves.

Notions: Smooth, contrasting colored yarn as markers or coilless safety pins. Yarn needle.

Gauge

(*Note:* These are steamed and "hung" gauges.)

For size 5, 3 reps (or 24 sts total) = 5" (12.5 cm) and 13 patt rows = 6" (15 cm) on size E hook.

For size 6, 4 reps (or 32 sts total) = 7" (18 cm) and 11 patt rows = 6" (15 cm) on size F hook.

For size 7, 3 reps (or 24 sts total) = 5½" (14 cm) and 10 patt rows = 6" (15 cm) on size G hook.

For size 8, 4 reps (or 32 sts total) = 7¾" (19.5 cm) and 8 patt rows = 6" (15 cm) on size H hook.

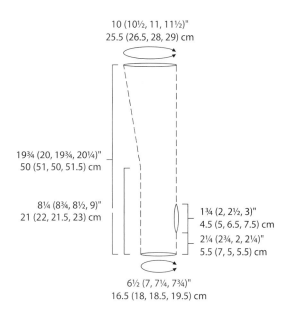

10 (10½, 11, 11½)"
25.5 (26.5, 28, 29) cm

19¾ (20, 19¾, 20¼)"
50 (51, 50, 51.5) cm

8¼ (8¾, 8½, 9)"
21 (22, 21.5, 23) cm

1¾ (2, 2½, 3)"
4.5 (5, 6.5, 7.5) cm

2¼ (2¾, 2, 2¼)"
5.5 (7, 5, 5.5) cm

6½ (7, 7¼, 7¾)"
16.5 (18, 18.5, 19.5) cm

Special Notes

- Each glove is worked in one piece circularly in the round to the thumb opening, where glove is worked back and forth, then glove is reconnected and worked in the round again.
- Stitch patterns are the same as for the sheath dress. Please refer to charts on page 94.

Special Stitches

V-st: (Dc, ch 1, dc) all in same st.

Shell st: 5 dc all in same ch-1 space.

Either V-st or Shell st will be referred to as units.

5-Row Increase Sequence (see chart on page 94):

Row 1: Work up to designated V-st, work 7-dc shell instead of 5-dc.

Row 2: Work up to 7-dc shell, skip first of these 7-dc, dc in 2nd dc, ch 1, dc in 4th dc, ch 1, dc in 6th dc, skip last of these 7-dc.

Row 3: Work up to dc's above 7-dc shell, 3-dc in first dc, dc in next dc, 3-dc in last dc.

Row 4: Work up to first of 3-dc shell of previous row, V-st in 2nd dc of 3-dc shell, 3-dc in dc, V-st in 2nd dc of next 3-dc shell.

Row 5: Work up to 3-dc shell of previous row, V-st in 2nd dc of this 3-dc shell.

Glove (make 2)

With designated hook for desired size, very loosely ch 32, join with sl st to first ch to form circle being careful not to twist.

Rnd 1 (RS) Ch 3: (counts as dc), work 2 more dc in same ch as sl st, *skip next 3 ch, V-st (or dc, ch 1, dc) into next ch, skip next 3 ch** Shell St (or 5 dc) in next ch; rep from * around, end last rep at **, work 2 more dc into same ch as joining sl st, join with sl st to top of beg ch-3, you are at inside edge and there are 8 units or 4 patt reps total.

Rnd 2 (WS): Ch 4 (counts as dc and ch-1) and turn, dc in same dc as sl st, *Shell St in ch-1 sp of next V-st**, V-st in 3rd dc of next Shell St; rep from * around, end last rep at **, join with sl st into 3rd ch of beg ch-4.

Rnd 3 (RS): Sl st into next ch-1 sp, turn, ch 3 (counts as dc), work 2 more dc in same ch as sl st, *V-st in 3rd dc of next Shell St**, Shell St in ch-1 sp of next V-st; rep from * around, end last rep at **, work 2 more dc into same ch-1 sp as beg sl st, join with sl st to top of beg ch-3.

Rep Rnds 2 and 3 for patt throughout (except when working in rows for thumb opening).

Rep Rnds 2 and 3 1 (1, 0, 0) times.

Separate for Thumb Opening

Next Row: Ch 3 (counts as dc), turn, (Shell St in next V-st; V-st in next Shell St) 3 times, Shell St in next V-st, dc in same dc as beg ch—7 units with dc at beg and end of row.

Next Row (RS): Ch 3 (counts as dc), turn, (V-st in next Shell St, Shell St in next V-st) 3 times, V-st in next Shell St, dc in top of ch-3 turning ch.

Next Row: Ch 3 (counts as dc), turn, (Shell St in next V-st; V-st in next Shell St) 3 times, Shell St in next V-st, dc in top of ch-3 turning ch.

Rejoin for Arm

Rejoining Rnd (RS): Ch 3 (counts as dc), turn, dc in first dc, (V-st in next Shell St, Shell St in next V-st) 3 times, V-st in next Shell St, 2 dc in last dc, ch 1, join with sl st to top of beg ch.

Next Rnd: Ch 4 (counts as dc and ch-1) and turn, dc in next ch-1 space, work as for Rnd 2 and after working 3 more units past beg ch-4 and dc, mark next unit for outside inc line, work rem rnd, join with sl st as before.

Rep Rnds 3 and 2 for patt of Shell Sts over V-sts and V-sts

over Shell Sts until 18 (16, 14, 10) rows total have been worked or work measures 8¼ (8¾, 8½, 9)" (20.5 [22, 21.5, 23] cm) ending with a V-st worked at outside inc line.

First Inc Sequence: Beg 5-row inc sequence at outside inc line on next row—10 units or 5 patt reps at end of last rnd.

Cont in patt until 27 (23, 21, 17) rows total have been worked or work measures 12½ (12½, 12½, 12¾)" (31.5 [31.5, 31.5, 32] cm) ending with a V-st worked at outside inc line.

Second Inc Sequence: Beg 5-row inc sequence at outside inc line on next row—12 units or 6 patt reps at end of last rnd.

Continue in patt until 43 (37, 33, 27) rows total have been worked or work measures 19¾ (20, 19¾, 20¼)" (50 [51, 50, 51.5] cm), fasten and end off.

NINE

Shell-Stitch Construction and Variations

The shell configuration has many variations. Shells can be solid, lacy, or both. You will find that a great many stitch patterns are nothing but a version of the shell. Learning to manipulate within its confines allows you to apply shapings to all of its many guises.

One way of changing shapes is to use half-shells effectively, as in the Scallops and Some Half-Shells Bolero and the Bollywood Tunic (pages 129 and 121, respectively). Another is to vary the number of stitches in each shell, as in Skirting the Issue on page 114 (the standard is 5, but you can use 3, 7, 9, or any odd number of stitches). Yet another option is to eliminate or gain a full shell altogether in a few steps, as in the Ensemble-Acting Tunic and Skirt (see pages 104 and 109, respectively).

On page 102 you will find a good "template" for shell stitches. Feel free to photocopy this page and draw your own shapes and patterns following the curving lines in this pattern family.

An even more accurate template is to put the shells onto a square grid where each square represents an inch. Using the gauge of the Scallops and Some Half-Shells Bolero, where 3 shells = 1 inch and 10 shell rows = 4 inches, the template on page 103 is to scale. This allows you to see all the dimensions of the garment as you outline the shells that you need.

Reduced sample of shell stitch pattern in rows

Shell template to scale

Ensemble-Acting Tunic and Skirt

Fully seamless and worked from the top down, both of these pieces feature
interior dart shaping. A finer-gauge yarn means bulk-free flattery,
and top-down construction means you can stop anytime:
choose your lengths as you go.

Tunic

Finished Size
Sizes S (M, L, 1X, 2X): 36 (38¼, 40½, 42¾, 45)" (91.5 [97,
103, 108.5, 114.5] cm) bust/chest circumference. This is a
standard-fitting garment. Sample is worked in size M.

Materials
Yarn: Jaeger Matchmaker Merino 4-ply (100% merino
wool, 200 yd [183 m]/50 g): #723 loden, 8 (9, 10,
11, 12) balls.

Crochet hook: Size D/3 (3.25 mm). Adjust hook size if
necessary to obtain the correct gauge.
Notions: Contrast-color scrap yarn for marking increases
and decreases.

Gauge
4 shells = 4½" (11.5 cm) or 1 shell = 1⅛" (3 cm) and 12
shell rows = 4" (10 cm). This is a steam-blocked gauge.

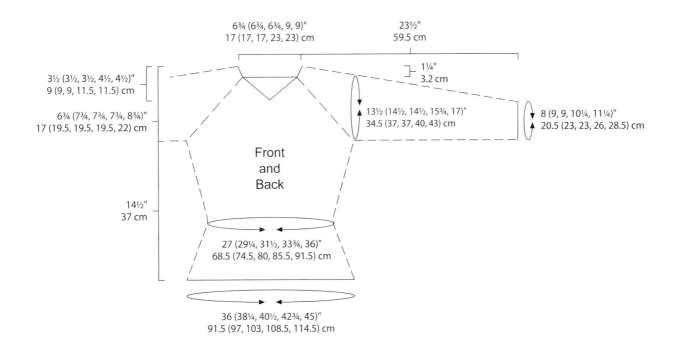

6¾ (6¾, 6¾, 9, 9)"
17 (17, 17, 23, 23) cm

23½"
59.5 cm

1¼"
3.2 cm

3½ (3½, 3½, 4½, 4½)"
9 (9, 9, 11.5, 11.5) cm

13½ (14½, 14½, 15¾, 17)"
34.5 (37, 37, 40, 43) cm

8 (9, 9, 10¼, 11¼)"
20.5 (23, 23, 26, 28.5) cm

6¾ (7¾, 7¾, 7¾, 8¾)"
17 (19.5, 19.5, 19.5, 22) cm

Front
and
Back

14½"
37 cm

27 (29¼, 31½, 33¾, 36)"
68.5 (74.5, 80, 85.5, 91.5) cm

36 (38¼, 40½, 42¾, 45)"
91.5 (97, 103, 108.5, 114.5) cm

Notes

- Tunic is worked from top down seamlessly, raglan style. Neck starts off back and forth, then is joined and worked in the round after neck opening is completed. Garment may be tried on in the process. Many shapings occur simultaneously, so keep careful track.

STITCH KEY

- • = sl st
- ◠ = chain (ch)
- + = single crochet (sc)
- | = double crochet (dc)
- = shell (5 dc)
- = large shell (7 dc)
- = small shell (3 dc)

Special Stitches

Shell: Sc in next sc (the center dc of previous 5-dc shell), skip 2 dc, 5 dc in next sc, skip 2 dc, sc in next st (the center dc of previous 5-dc shell).

Large Shell: Sc in next sc (the center dc of previous 5-dc shell), skip 2 dc, 7 dc in next sc, skip 2 dc, sc in next st (the center dc of previous 5-dc shell).

Small Shell: Sc in next sc, skip 1 dc, 3 dc in next dc (the center dc of previous 7-dc shell), skip 1 dc, sc in next st (the center dc of previous 5-dc shell).

Expanded Shell: At beginning of row, ch 4 (counts as a trc) and turn, work 2 trc and 3 dc in first trc. At end of row, work 3 dc and 3 trc all in top of beg ch-4.

3-Row Increase Sequence:

Row 1: Work Large Shell in designated sc.

Row 2: Shell in sc at start of Large Shell, skip 1 dc, sc in next dc, skip 1 dc, 3 dc in next dc for Small Shell, skip 1 dc, sc in next dc, skip 1 dc, Shell in sc at end of Large Shell.

Row 3: Shell in sc, sc in center of Small Shell, Shell in sc.

3-Row Decrease Sequence

Row 1: Work Small Shell in designated sc.

Row 2: Work Small Shell in sc on each side of Small Shell.

Row 3: Work up to Small Shells ending with 5 dc in sc before first Small Shell, skip next dc, pull up lp in next dc (center of first Small Shell), skip dc-sc-dc, pull up lp in next dc (center of second Small Shell), yo hook and draw through all 3 loops on hook to dec both Small Shells tog into one (counts as sc), skip next dc, 5 dc in next sc.

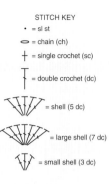

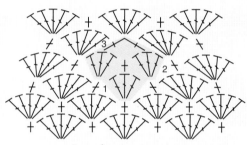

3-row increase sequence

3-row decrease sequence

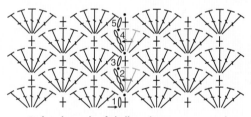

Reduced sample of shell stitch pattern in rounds

Shell St in the Round

Row 1: Ch 1 and turn, sc in first dc, * skip next 2 dc, 5-dc in next sc, skip next 2 dc, sc in next dc; rep from * ending without last sc but with sl st to first sc to join.

Row 2: Ch 3 (counts as dc) and turn, dc in sl st at base of ch, * skip next 2 dc, sc in next dc, skip next 2 dc, 5-dc in next sc; rep from ending with only 3 dc in dc at base of beg ch, join with sl st to top of beg ch-3 turning ch.

Rep Rows 1 and 2.

Yoke

Loosely ch 71 (71, 71, 83, 83).

Row 1 (WS): Work 2 trc and 3 dc in 5th ch from hook, * skip 2 ch, sc in next ch, skip 2 ch, 5 dc in next ch; rep from *, end with not 5-dc in last ch but instead 3 dc and 3 trc = 10 (10, 10, 12, 12) regular 5-dc Shells and 2 Expanded Shells at each end.

Row 2 (RS): Ch 4 (counts as a trc) and turn, work 2 trc and 3 dc in first trc, [skip 2 sts, sc in next st, skip 2 sts, 7 dc in next st] 3 times, [skip 2 sts, sc in next st, skip 2 sts, 5 dc in next st] 2 (2, 2, 3, 3) times, skip 2 sts, sc in next st, skip 2 sts, 7 dc in next st, [skip 2 sts, sc in next st, skip 2 sts, 5 dc in next st] 2 (2, 2, 3, 3) times, [skip 2 sts, sc in next st, skip 2 sts, 7 dc in next st] 3 times, skip 2 sts, sc in next st, skip 2 sts, end with 3 dc and 3 trc all in top of beg ch-4—one Expanded Side Shell, three 7-dc Large Shells, 2 (2, 2, 3, 3) 5-dc Shells, one 7-dc Large Shell, 2 (2, 2, 3, 3) 5-dc Shells, three 7-dc Large Shells, and an Expanded Side Shell.

Mark first Large Shell as Raglan Line, next Large Shell as Center-Sleeve Line, next Large Shell as Raglan Line, next Large Shell as Center-Back Line, next Large Shell as Raglan Line, next Large Shell as Center-Sleeve Line, and Large Shell as Raglan Line. All inc's will continue vertically down these same lines of shells. Basically, cont all 3-row Increase Sequences and beg new ones at each Raglan Line every 3rd row or immediately after each completed one 5 (6, 6, 6, 7) times total, beg new ones at each Center-Sleeve Line on Rows/Rnds 5 and 8 (5 and 8, 5 and 8, 5 and 8 and 11, 5 and 8 and 11), beg new ones at Center-Back Line on Rows/Rnds 5 and 8 (5 and 10, 5 and 8 and 11, 5 and 8, 5 and 8), and at Center-Front Line on Rnds 8 (10, 8 and 11, -, -). The next few rows are spelled out as foll:

Row 3: Ch 4 (counts as a trc) and turn, work 2 trc and 3 dc in first trc, skip 2 sts, sc in next st, skip 2 sts, [5 dc in next st, skip 1 st, sc in next st, skip 1 st, 3 dc in next st, skip 1 st, sc in next dc, skip 1 st] 3 times, *[5 dc in next st, skip 2 sts, sc in next st, skip 2 sts] 2 (2, 2, 3, 3) times, 5 dc in next st, skip 1 st, sc in next st, skip 1 st, 3 dc in next st, skip 1 st, sc in next st, skip 1 st *, rep from * to *, [5 dc in next st, skip 1 st, sc in next st, skip 1 st, 3 dc in next st, skip 1 st] 2 times, 5 dc in next st, skip 2 sts, sc in next st, skip 2 sts, end with 3 dc and 3 trc all in top of beg ch-4 = Expanded Side Shell, 5-dc Shell, 3-dc Small Shell, 5-dc Shell, 3-dc Small Shell, 5-dc Shell, 3-dc Small Shell, 3 (3, 3, 4, 4) 5-dc Shells, 3-dc Small Shell, 3 (3, 3, 4, 4) 5-dc Shells, 3-dc Small Shell, 5-dc Shell, 3-dc Small Shell, 5-dc Shell, 3-dc Small Shell, 5-dc Shell, and an Expanded Side Shell.

Row 4: Ch 4 (counts as a trc) and turn, work 2 trc and 3 dc in first trc, [skip 2 sts, sc in next st, skip 2 sts, 5 dc in next st] 2 times, [skip 1 st, sc in next st or center dc of sm-shell, skip 1 st, 5 dc in next sc, skip 2 sts, sc in next st, skip 2 sts, 5 dc in next sc] 3 times, [skip 2 sts, sc in next st, skip 2 sts, 5 dc in next st] 2 (2, 2, 3, 3) times, [skip 1 st, sc in next st or center dc of sm-shell, skip 1 st, 5 dc in next sc, skip 2 sts, sc in next st, skip 2 sts, 5 dc in next sc], [skip 2 sts, sc in next st, skip 2 sts, 5 dc in next st] 2 (2, 2, 3, 3) times, [skip 1 st, sc in next st or center dc of sm-shell, skip 1 st, 5 dc in next sc, skip 2 sts, sc in next st, skip 2 sts, 5 dc in next sc] 3 times, skip 2 sts, sc in next st, skip 2 sts, end with 3 dc and 3 trc all in top of beg ch-4—20 (20, 20, 22, 22) 5-dc Shells and an Expanded Side Shell at each end.

Row 5: Ch 4 (counts as a trc) and turn, work 2 trc and 3 dc in first trc, work in Shell st patt but work 7-dc Large Shells at all Increase Lines, end with Expanded Side Shell.

Cont to work Expanded Side Shells at beg and end of rows, cont with inc's at Increase Lines.

At beg and end of Row 7 (7, 7, 10, 10), work regular shells instead of Expanded Shells, then join with sl st to top of beg ch-4 turning ch. From now on, work in rounds, beg with Row 2 of Shell St in the Round directions, working into sl st as if it were a sc. *Note:* This sl st marks the Center Increase line.

Cont to work est patt until there are 16 (19, 19, 19, 22) rows/rnds total. There are 14 (15, 16, 17, 18) Shells for each Front and Back and 10 (11, 11, 12, 12) Shells for each Sleeve for 48 (52, 54, 58, 62) Shells total. Work one row even in patt for 17 (20, 20, 20, 23) rows/rnds total.

Body

Next Rnd: Keep to Shell patt ending with sc in center dc of Shell at next Raglan Line, ch 11, sc in center dc of Shell at next Raglan Line, cont in est Shell patt ending with sc in center dc of Shell at next Raglan Line, ch 11, sc in center dc of Shell at next Raglan Line, cont in est Shell patt and complete row.

Next Rnd: Keep to Shell patt ending with 5-dc Shell in sc atop center dc of Shell at next Raglan Line, *skip next 2 ch, sc in next ch, skip next 2 ch *, 5-dc Shell in next ch and mark this Shell as Side-Line; rep from * to *, work 5-dc Shell in sc atop center dc of Shell at next Raglan Line, cont in est Shell patt ending with 5-dc Shell in sc atop center dc of Shell at next Raglan Line, ** skip next 2 ch, sc in next ch, skip next 2 ch **, 5-dc Shell in next ch and mark this Shell as Side-Line; rep from ** to **, work 5-dc Shell in sc atop center dc of Shell at next Raglan Line, cont in est Shell patt and complete row.

Work in rounds on these 32 (34, 36, 38, 40) Body Shells until 28 (29, 29, 29, 30) rows/rnds total have been worked, marking center 6 (7, 8, 9, 10) shells of Front and Back on an even (odd, odd, odd, even) row.

Shape Sides
At Side Lines, beg 3-Row Decrease Sequence on next rnd and on rnd 38 (39, 39, 39, 40).

Shape Darts
AT THE SAME TIME, work until 38 (39, 39, 39, 40) rows/rnds total have been completed.

Next Rnd: [Work up to sc before marked center Shells, beg 3-Row Decrease Sequence in next sc, work to sc after marked center Shells, beg 3-Row Decrease Sequence in next sc] twice.

After all Side and Dart decs have been completed, work even on 24 (26, 28, 30, 32) shells until 45 (46, 46, 46, 47) rows/rnds total have been worked.

Beg 3-Row Increase Sequence over previous Decrease Sequences.

Shape Sides

AT THE SAME TIME, after 44 (45, 45, 45, 46) rows/rnds total have been worked, beg 3-Row Increase Sequence on next rnd and on Rnd 52 (53, 53, 53, 54) at Side Lines. Work in rounds on these 32 (34, 36, 38, 40) Body Shells until 60 (63, 63, 63, 66) rows/rnds total have been worked. Fasten and end off.

Sleeves

Next Rnd: With RS (WS, WS, WS, RS) facing, beg at underarm and join yarn to underside of 6th ch, ch 1 and sc in same ch, *skip next 2 ch, 5-dc Shell in underside of next ch, skip next 2 ch *, sc in center dc of Shell at next Raglan Line, cont in est Shell pattern ending with sc in center dc of Shell at next Raglan Line, rep from * to *, join with sl st to first sc.

Work in rounds on these 12 (13, 13, 14, 15) Sleeve Shells and cont to mark Center-Sleeve Line. Beg 3-Row Decrease Sequence on Rnd 26 (27, 27, 27, 26), Rnd 35 (36, 36, 36, 35), Rnd 44 (45, 45, 45, 44), Rnd 53 (54, 54, 54, 53), and on Rnd 62 (63, 63, 63, 62), having one less Shell after completing each Decrease Sequence. Work even on 7 (8, 8, 9, 10) shells until 71 rnds total have been completed or to desired length. Fasten and end off.

Finishing

Steam-block piece to measurements and to smooth and even out increases and decreases.

Neck Trim

With RS facing, join to center back neck, ch 1, sc in same space as join, sc evenly around whole neck, join with sl st to beg sc, fasten and end off.

Skirt

Finished Size

Sizes S (M, L, 1X, 2X): 24¾ (27, 29¼, 31½, 33¾)" (63 [68.5, 74.5, 80, 85.5] cm) waist circumference. This is a close-fitting garment. Skirt shown measures 27" (68.5 cm).

Materials

Yarn: Jaeger Matchmaker Merino 4-ply (100% merino wool, 200 yd [183 m]/50 g): #723 loden, 6 (6, 7, 7, 8) balls.

Crochet hook: Size D/3 (3.25 mm). Adjust hook size if necessary to obtain the correct gauge.

Notions: Four ⅝" buttons. Contrast-color scrap yarn for marking increases.

Gauge

4 shells = 4½" (11.5 cm) and 12 shell rows = 4" (10 cm) when steam-blocked.

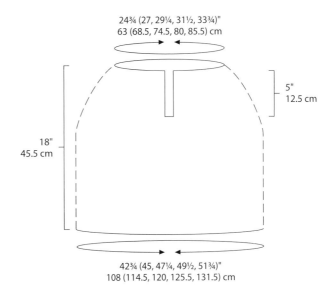

24¾ (27, 29¼, 31½, 33¾)"
63 (68.5, 74.5, 80, 85.5) cm

5"
12.5 cm

18"
45.5 cm

42¾ (45, 47¼, 49½, 51¾)"
108 (114.5, 120, 125.5, 131.5) cm

Notes

- Skirt is worked from top down seamlessly. Waist starts off back and forth, then is joined and worked in the round after button opening is completed. Garment may be tried on in the process.

Special Stitches

Shell: Sc in next st (the center dc of previous 5-dc shell), sk 2 dc, 5 dc in next sc, sk 2 dc, sc in next st (the center dc of previous 5-dc shell).

Large Shell: Sc in next st (the center dc of previous 5-dc shell), sk 2 dc, 7 dc in next sc, sk 2 dc, sc in next st (the center dc of previous 5-dc shell).

Small Shell: Sc in next st, sk 1 dc, 3 dc in next dc (the center dc of previous 7-dc shell), sk 1 dc, sc in next st.

3-Row Increase Sequence:

Row 1: Work Large Shell in designated sc.

Row 2: Shell in sc at start of Large Shell, sk 1 dc, sc in next dc, sk 1 dc, 3 dc in next dc for Small Shell, sk 1 dc, sc in next dc, sk 1 dc, Shell in sc at end of Large Shell.

Row 3: Shell in sc, sc in center of Small Shell, Shell in sc.

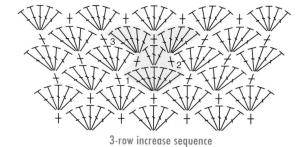

3-row increase sequence

Shell St in the Round:

Row 1 (WS): Ch 1 and turn, sc in first dc, *sk 2 dc, 5-dc in next sc, sk 2 dc, sc in next dc; rep from * ending without last sc but with sl st to first sc to join.

Row 2 (RS): Ch 3 (counts as dc) and turn, dc in sl st at base of ch, *sk 2 dc, sc in next dc, sk 2 dc, 5-dc in next sc; rep from * ending with only 3 dc in dc at base of beg ch, join with sl st to top of beg ch-3 turning ch.

Rep Rows 1 and 2.

Body

Waist

Loosely ch 128 (140, 152, 164, 176).

Row 1: Sc in 2nd ch from hook, *sk 2 ch, 5 dc in next ch, sk 2 ch, sc in next ch; rep from *—21 (23, 25, 27, 29) shells.

Row 2: Ch 3 (counts as a dc) and turn, work 2 more dc in first sc, [sk 2 dc, sc in next dc, sk 2 dc, 5 dc in next sc] across, end with sk 2 dc, 3 dc in last sc—20 (22, 24, 26, 28) shells with a half-shell at each end.

Row 3: Ch 1 and turn, sc in first dc, [sk 2 dc, 5 dc in next sc, sk 2 dc, sc in next dc] across.

Row 4: Rep Row 2, marking shells with contrasting yarn for Increase Lines as follows: for size S, mark 2nd, 8th, 13th, and 19th whole shells for Darts, and 5th and 16th for Sides; for size L, mark 3rd, 9th, 16th, and 22nd whole shells for Darts, and 6th and 19th for Sides; for size 2X, mark 4th, 10th, 19th, and 25th whole shells for Darts, and 7th and 22nd for Sides.

Row 5: Rep Row 3, marking shells with contrasting yarn for Increase Lines as follows: for size M, mark 3rd, 9th, 15th, and 21st shells for Darts, and 6th and 18th shells for Sides; for size 1X, mark 4th, 10th, 18th, and 24th shells for Darts, and 7th and 21st shells for Sides.

Row 6: Work in patt as per Row 2, but for sizes S (L, 2X), work 7-dc Large Shell at sc of each Side Increase Line.

Row 7: Work in patt as per Row 3, but for sizes S (L, 2X), continue inc sequence with a 3-dc Small Shell at center of Large Shell at each Side Increase Line; for sizes M (1X), work 7-dc Large Shell at sc of each Side Increase Line.

Row 8: Work in Shell st patt, but for sizes S (L, 2X), complete inc sequence at each Side Increase Line, at

the same time work 7-dc Large Shell at each Dart Increase Line—23 (27, 31) shells; for sizes M (1X), continue inc sequence with a 3-dc Small Shell at center of Large Shell at each Side Increase Line.

Row 9: Work in Shell st patt, but for sizes S (L, 2X), continue inc sequence with a 3-dc Small Shell at center of Large Shell at each Dart Increase Line; for sizes M (1X), complete inc sequence at each Side Increase Line, and at same time work 7-dc Large Shell at each Dart Increase Line—25 (29) shells.

Row 10: Work in Shell st patt, but for sizes S (L, 2X), complete inc sequence at each Dart Increase Line—27 (31, 35) shells; for sizes M (1X), continue inc sequence with a 3-dc Small Shell at center of Large Shell at each Dart Increase Line.

Row 11: Work in Shell st patt, but for sizes M (1X), complete inc sequence at each Dart Increase Line—29 (33) shells.

Cont to work in Shell st patt, working inc sequences at Side Increase Lines beg with 7-dc Large Shells on Row 13 (14, 13, 14, 13) and on Row 20 (21, 20, 21, 20).

AT THE SAME TIME, work inc sequences at Dart Increase Lines beg with 7-dc Large Shells on row 15 (16, 15, 16, 15).

AT THE SAME TIME, at end of Row 15, join ends to form a circle as follows: after last sc, ch 5, join with sl st to first sc to form a circle. On next row, beg Row 2 of Shell St in the round, working into ch's as if they were regular sts. Cont to work in Shell St in the round hereafter.

Row 23: Locate center Back (directly beneath ch-5 at base of button opening) and center Front, and work 7-dc Large Shell in sc at each of these centers; complete inc sequence on Rows 24 and 25.

Cont to work in Shell St in the Round on 38 (40, 42, 44, 46) shells until piece measures 18" (45 cm) total or to desired length.

Finishing

Steam-block piece to measurements and to smooth and even out increases.

Button Band: With RS facing, sc evenly spaced along left edge of opening. Work 4 more rows of sc. Fasten and end off. Mark for 4 evenly spaced buttons.

Buttonhole Band: With RS facing, sc along right edge of opening same number of sts evenly spaced as for Button Band. Work another row of sc.

Row 3 (buttonhole row): Sc across, working (ch 2, sk 2 sc) for each marked button of corresponding Button Band.

Row 4: Sc across and in each ch of ch-2 buttonholes.

Row 5: Sc across. Fasten and end off.

Sew side edges of both Button Band and Buttonhole Band to chain sts of Row 15. Sew buttons to marked Button-band.

Trim: With RS facing, sc along underside of beg foundation ch. Turn and sl st into each sc across. Fasten and end off.

Skirting the Issue

Light as air and drapey as sin, you'll find this a wardrobe staple. Pair it with a crisp white shirt, a cropped jacket, even a T-shirt. Boots, strappy sandals, or ballerina flats complete the look. The waist is shaped by reducing the shell-stitch motif from 5 to 3 stitches.

Finished Sizes

Full Hips: 38¹/₂ (40¹/₂, 42, 44, 46, 47¹/₂)", Waist = 28 (29¹/₂, 30³/₄, 32, 33¹/₂, 34³/₄)", Total length with trim = 27" (68.5 cm).

Materials

Yarn: Cascade/Madil Kid Seta (70% kid mohair, 30% silk; 230 yd [211 m]/25 g), #837 midnight, 6 (7, 8, 9, 10) skeins.

Crochet hook: Size F/5 (3.75 mm). Adjust hook size if necessary to obtain the correct gauge.

Notions: One ⁵/₈" (1.5 cm) button.

Gauge

(Sc, 5-dc shell, sc, ch 5) 3 times = 5¹/₂" (14 cm) and one 4-row repeat = 2" (5 cm) in Shell Mesh pattern.

(Sc, 3-dc shell, sc, ch 3) 4 times = 5¹/₂" (14 cm) in Mini-Shell Mesh pattern above hips.

18 sc = 4" (10 cm) in Waistband pattern.

Note

• Always work with 2 strands held together. Skirt is worked from bottom up, then trim is worked downwards from foundation chain.

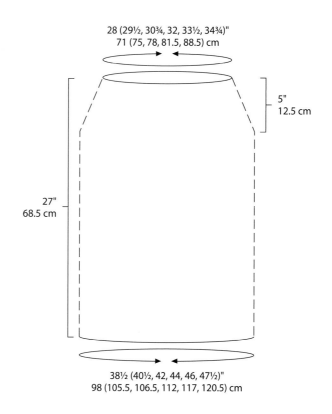

28 (29½, 30¾, 32, 33½, 34¾)"
71 (75, 78, 81.5, 88.5) cm

5"
12.5 cm

27"
68.5 cm

38½ (40½, 42, 44, 46, 47½)"
98 (105.5, 106.5, 112, 117, 120.5) cm

Special Stitches

Picot: Ch 3, insert hook into front lp of last sc and into side lp of same last sc and work sl st.

Shell Mesh Pattern

With 2 strands held together throughout, loosely ch a multiple of 10 sts, join with sl st in first ch to form circle, being careful not to twist ch.

Rnd 1 (WS): Ch 1 and turn, sc in same ch as joining sl st, ch 5, sk next 4 ch, *sc in next ch, ch 5, sk next 4 ch; rep from * across, join with sl st to first sc.

Rnd 2 (RS): Ch 3 and turn (counts as a dc), work 2 more dc in same sc as joining sl st, *sc in center ch of next ch-5 lp, ch 5, sc in center ch of next ch-5 lp, sk next 2 ch**, 5 dc in next sc; rep from * around,

ending last rep at **, work 2 more dc in first sc, join with sl st to top of turning ch.

Rnd 3: Ch 1 and turn, sc in first dc, *ch 5, sc in center ch of next ch-5 lp**, ch 5, sc in center dc of next 5-dc; rep from * around, ending last rep at **, ch 2, dc into first sc.

Rnd 4: Ch 1 and turn, sc in last dc of previous rnd, *sk next 2 ch, 5 dc in next sc, sc in center ch of next ch-5 lp**, ch 5, sc in center ch of next ch-5 lp; rep from * around, ending last rep at **, ch 2, dc into first sc.

Rnd 5: Ch 1 and turn, sc in last dc of previous rnd, *ch 5, sc in center dc of next 5-dc, ch 5**, sc in center ch of next ch-5 lp; rep from * around, ending last rep at **, join with sl st to first sc.

Rep Rnds 2–5 for patt.

STITCH KEY
- ⌒ = chain (ch)
- • = slip stitch (sl st)
- + = single crochet (sc)
- ┼ = double crochet (dc)
- ⬚ = picot

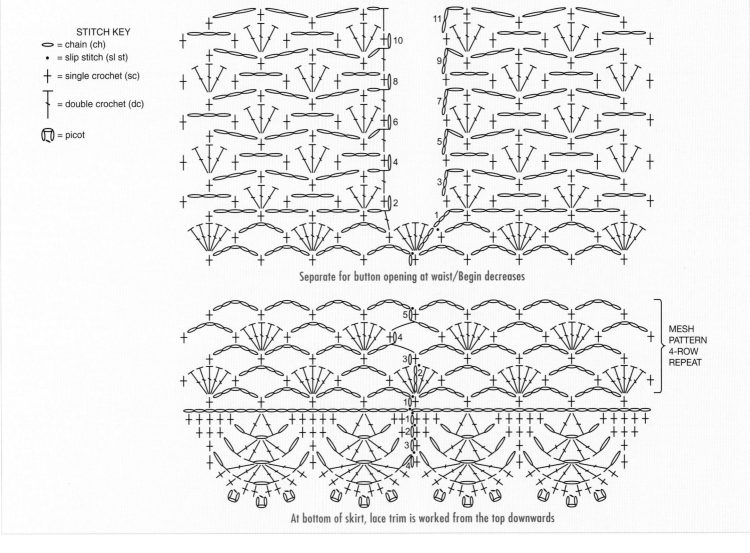

Separate for button opening at waist/Begin decreases

MESH PATTERN 4-ROW REPEAT

At bottom of skirt, lace trim is worked from the top downwards

116

Skirt

With 2 strands held together throughout, loosely ch 210 (220, 230, 240, 250, 260, 270), join with sl st to first ch to form circle, being careful not to twist ch.

Work Rnd 1 of Shell Mesh pattern—42 (44, 46, 48, 50, 52) ch-5 lps.

Continue to work Shell Mesh pattern until piece measures 22" (56 cm) from beginning or desired length (make any length adjustments here), ending with a patt Rnd 5.

Next Rnd (RS): Ch 3 and turn (counts as a dc), 4 more dc in same sc as joining sl st, *sk next 2 ch, sc in center ch of next ch-5 lp, ch 5, sc in center ch of next ch-5 lp**, sk next 2 ch, 5 dc in next sc; rep from * across, ending last rep at **, join with sl st to top of beg ch.

Separate for Opening/Beg Decreases

Row 1 (WS): Ch 4 and turn (counts as a dc and ch 1), sc in center ch of first ch-5 lp, *ch 3 only, sc in center dc of next 5-dc, ch 3 only, sc in center ch of next ch-5 lp; rep from * across to last ch-5 lp, ending with ch 1, dc in next sc, do not work over rem 4 dc but leave empty for buttonhole/buttonband later. From here on, do not join rnds.

Row 2 (RS): Ch 1 and turn, sc in first dc, *3 dc only in next sc**, sc in center ch of next ch-3 lp, ch 3, sc in center ch of next ch-3 lp; rep from * across, ending last rep at **, sc in 3rd ch of beg ch 4.

Row 3: Ch 4 and turn (counts as a dc and ch 1), *sc in center dc of next 3-dc**, ch 3, sc in center ch of next ch-3 lp, ch 3; rep from * across, ending last rep at **, ch 1, dc in last sc.

Row 4: Ch 1 and turn, sc in first dc, *ch 3, sc in center ch of next ch-3 lp, 3 dc in next sc, sc in center ch of next ch-3 lp; rep from * across, ending with ch 3, sc in 3rd ch of beg ch 4.

Row 5: Ch 4 and turn (counts as a dc and ch 1), sc in center ch of first ch-3 lp, *ch 3, sc in center dc of next 3-dc, ch 3, sc in center ch of next ch-3 lp; rep from * across, ending with ch 1, dc in last sc.

Rows 6–10: Rep Rows 2–5, then rep Row 2 again.

Row 11 (WS): Ch 3 and turn (counts as a hdc and ch 2), *sc in center dc of next 3-dc**, ch 2 only, sc in center ch of next ch-3 lp, ch 2 only; rep from * across, ending last rep at **, ch 1, hdc in last sc, fasten and end off.

Waistband and Buttonhole/Buttonband

Row 1: With RS facing, join yarn and sc evenly along left side edge of opening, ch 1 for corner, sc in each st across top of Row 11, ch 1 for corner, sc evenly along right edge of opening.

Row 2 (WS): Ch 1 and turn, sc in each sc around working [sc, ch 1, sc] in ch-1 space of each corner.

Row 3 (Buttonhole row): Rep Row 2, working buttonhole at first corner only as follows: sk sc before ch-1 space, ch 3 for buttonhole, sk ch-1 space and sc after ch-1 space.

Row 4: Ch 1 and turn, sc in each sc around working [sc, ch 1, sc] in ch-1 space of first corner and [2 sc, ch 1, 2 sc] in last ch-3 corner lp to complete buttonhole.

Row 5: Ch 1 and turn, sc in each sc and ch-1 space around without working extra sts in corners.

Row 6: Turn and sl st in each sc around, fasten and end off leaving 6" (15 cm) tail.

Using tail, sew both side edges of Buttonhole/Buttonband to bottom of opening with buttonhole band on top. Sew button to buttonband to correspond to buttonhole.

Bottom Trim

With RS facing, attach yarn to opposite side of foundation ch in ch at base of any sc with a 5-dc shell below it.

Rnd 1: Ch 1, sc in same space as joining sl st, *2 sc in next ch space, ch 1, [dc, ch 1, dc] all in next foundation ch at base of next sc, ch 1, 2 sc in next ch space**, sc in next foundation ch at base of next sc; rep from * around, ending last rep at **, join with sl st to beg sc—21 (22, 23, 24, 25, 26) "fans."

Rnd 2: Ch 1, sc in same sc as joining sl st, *sc in next sc, ch 1, sk next (sc, ch-1 space and dc), [2 dc, ch 1, 2 dc] all in next ch-1 space, ch 1, sk next (dc, ch-1 space and sc)**, sc in each of next 2 sc; rep from * around, ending last rep at **, sc in next sc, join with sl st to beg sc.

Rnd 3: Ch 1, sc in same sc as joining sl st, *ch 1, sk next (sc, ch-1 space and 2 dc), [3 dc, ch 1, 3 dc] all in next ch-1 space, ch 1, sk next (2 dc, ch-1 space and sc)**, sc in next sc; rep from * around, ending last rep at **, join with sl st to beg sc.

Rnd 4: Ch 1 and turn, sc in same sc as joining sl st, *sk next ch-1 space, sc in each of next 2 dc, picot, sc in next dc, [sc, picot, sc] in next ch-1 space, sc in next dc, picot, sc in each of next 2 dc, sk next ch-1 space **, sc in next sc; rep from * around, ending last rep at **, join with sl st to beg sc, fasten and end off.

Bollywood Tunic

Amazingly stretchy, this fabric molds to accommodate any shape. Body and sleeves
are worked in the round so as not to interrupt the lace pattern. Beads add extra
texture and sparkle, and are prestrung on the yarn.

Finished Size

Sizes S (M, L, 1X, 2X): 28¾ (32, 35¼, 38½, 41½)" (73
[81.5, 90, 98, 105.5] cm) bust/chest circumference. This is
a tight-fitting garment. Sample was done in size S.

Materials

Yarn: Lily Chin Signature Collection Gramercy (100%
superwash merino wool, 127 yd [116 m]/50 g):
#5002 black, 5 (5, 6, 6, 7) balls.

Crochet hook: Size G/6 (4 mm). Adjust hook size if
necessary to obtain the correct gauge.
Notions: Beading needle. Acrylic faceted beads, size
6mm, red, 865 (985, 1065, 1140, 1250) beads.

Gauge

5 mesh sts and 8 mesh rows = 4" (10 cm) unstretched. This
is a very springy and stretchy fabric.

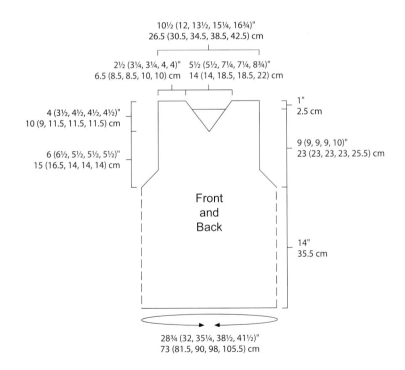

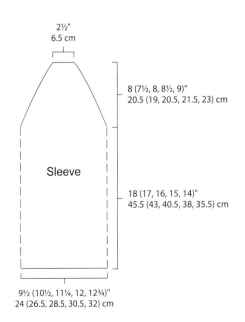

Notes

- Prestring beads onto yarn before working (about 150 beads per ball). If more beads are necessary, string from end of ball and move forwards/upwards.
- Body and Sleeves are worked in the round. Armholes and Sleeve Caps are worked flat.

Special Stitches

Bsc (beaded single crochet): Pick up lp in st, bring bead up yarn and snuggle behind hook, yarn around hook and draw through 2 lps on hook to complete st. Bead will lie on yarn strand behind sc (on RS of fabric, if Bsc is worked on WS).

Mesh st: Ch-5 loop with sc before and after this.

Half-Mesh st: Dc and ch-2 at beg of row or ch-2 and dc at end of row.

```
STITCH KEY
⌒ = chain (ch)
•  = slip stitch (sl st)
✝  = single crochet (sc)
♦  = beaded single crochet (Bsc)
🕇  = double crochet (dc)
```

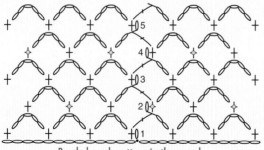

Beaded mesh pattern in the round

Beaded Mesh Pattern in the Round:

Ch a multiple of 8. Join in a circle, being careful not to twist.

Rnd 1 (RS): Ch 1, sc in same ch as sl st, *ch 5, sk 3 ch, sc in next ch; rep from * across, end ch 2, sk 3 ch, dc into first sc.

Rnd 2 (WS): Ch 1 and turn, Bsc in dc, *ch 5, sc in 3rd (center) ch of next ch-5 lp **, ch 5, Bsc in 3rd (center) ch of next ch-5 lp*; rep from * to * across, end last rep at **, ch 2, dc in first sc.

Rnd 3 (RS): Ch 1 and turn, sc in dc, *ch 5, sc in 3rd (center) ch of next ch-5 lp; rep from *, end ch 2, dc in first sc.

Rnd 4 (WS): Ch 1 and turn, sc in dc, *ch 5, Bsc in 3rd (center) ch of next ch-5 lp **, ch 5, sc in 3rd (center) ch of next ch-5 lp*; rep from * to * across, end last rep at **, ch 2, dc in first sc.

Rnd 5 (RS): Rep Rnd 3.

Rep Rnds 2–5 for patt.

Mesh Pattern Flat:

Row 1: Ch 1 and turn, sc in 1st st, *ch 5, sc in 3rd (center) ch of next ch-5 lp, rep from * across.

Row 2: Ch 5 (counts as a dc and ch-2) and turn (counts as Half-Mesh st), *sc in 3rd (center) ch of next ch-5 lp, ch 5, rep from * across, end sc in 3rd (center) ch of last ch-5 lp, ch 2, dc in last sc (counts as Half-Mesh st).

Rep Rows 1 and 2 for patt, working Bsc instead of sc (except at side edges) on WS rows as necessary to maintain beading patt est by Beaded Mesh Pattern in the Round.

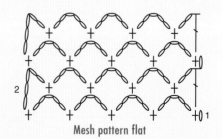

Mesh pattern flat

Body

Loosely ch 144 (160, 176, 192, 208). Begin Beaded
Mesh Pattern in the Round—36 (40, 44, 48, 52) Mesh
sts.
Continue in Beaded Mesh Pattern in the Round until
piece measures 14" (35.5 cm) or 28 rnds total, ending
with a WS beading row.

Shape Back Armholes

Next Row (RS, dec row): Work Row 1 of Mesh Pattern
Flat, working only 16 (18, 20, 22, 24) Mesh Sts
and ending with sc, then end with ch 2, dc in
center ch of next ch-5 lp, leaving rem sts to be
worked for Front Armholes—17 (19, 21, 23, 25)
Mesh Sts total.

Next Row (WS, dec row): Rep last row, working only
15 (17, 19, 21, 23) Mesh Sts—16 (18, 20, 22, 24)
Mesh Sts total.

Rep last 2 rows once, working 1 less Mesh St each row—
14 (16, 18, 20, 22) Mesh Sts total.

Next Row (RS, dec row): Work Row 1 of Mesh Pattern
Flat, working 13 (15, 17, 19, 21) Mesh Sts and
ending with sc.

Work Row 2 of Mesh Pattern Flat, then cont to work in
Mesh Pattern Flat until piece measures 22½ (22½, 22½,
22½, 23½)" (57 [57, 57, 57, 59.5] cm) or 45 (45, 45, 45,
47) rows total have been completed; end ready to work
a WS row.

Shape Back Neck and Left Shoulder

Next Row (WS): Keeping to Mesh Pattern Flat, work
2½ (3½, 3½, 4½, 4½) Mesh Sts, ch 2, dc in center
ch of next ch-5 lp.

Next Row (RS): Ch 1 and turn, work 3 (4, 4, 5, 5)
Mesh Sts across, fasten and end off.

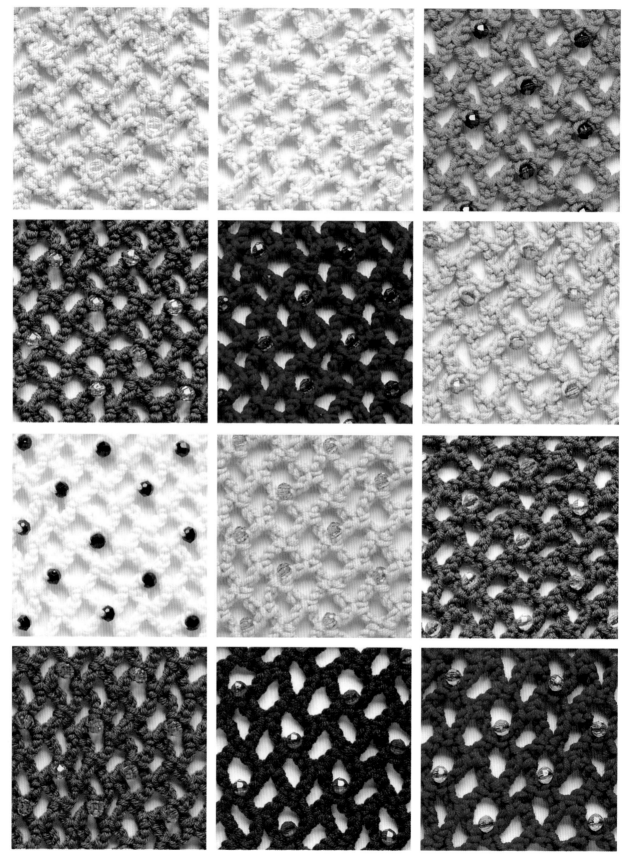

Sample combinations of beads and yarn colors.

Shape Right Shoulder

With WS facing, sk center 5 (5, 7, 7, 9) loops past last worked loop, join yarn to center ch of next ch-5 lp, ch 1, sc in same ch as join, work remaining $3\frac{1}{2}$ ($4\frac{1}{2}$, $4\frac{1}{2}$, $5\frac{1}{2}$, $5\frac{1}{2}$) Mesh Sts.

Next Row (RS): Ch 1 and turn, work 3 (4, 4, 5, 5) Mesh Sts across, fasten and end off.

Shape Front Armholes

Next Row (RS): With RS facing, join yarn to center ch of next ch-5 lp after loop worked into for Back Armhole, ch 1, sc in same ch as join, work as for Back Armhole until piece measures 20 (20, 19, 19, 19)" (51 [51, 48.5, 48.5, 48.5] cm) or 40 (40, 38, 38, 38) rows total have been completed; end ready to work a RS row.

Shape Front Neck and Right Shoulder

Next Row (RS, dec row): Ch 1 and turn, work 5 (6, 7, 8, 9) Mesh Sts across, ch 2, dc in center ch of next ch-5 lp—6 (7, 8, 9, 10) Mesh Sts total.

Next Row (WS, dec row): Work Row 1 of Mesh Pattern Flat—$5\frac{1}{2}$ ($6\frac{1}{2}$, $7\frac{1}{2}$, $8\frac{1}{2}$, $9\frac{1}{2}$) Mesh Sts.

Rep last 2 rows with one-half less Mesh St each row until 3 (4, 4, 5, 5) Mesh Sts rem.

Next Row: Work Row 2 of Mesh Pattern Flat—2 (3, 3, 4, 4) Mesh Sts with a Half-Mesh St at each end, fasten and end off.

Shape Left Shoulder

Next Row (RS): With RS facing, sk ch-5 lp after loop worked into for Left Shoulder, join yarn to center ch of next ch-5 lp, ch 1, sc in same ch as join, work remaining 6 (7, 8, 9, 10) Mesh Sts.

Next Row (WS): Ch 1 and turn, work Half-Mesh St at beg of row, then 4 (5, 6, 7, 8) Mesh Sts, ch 2, dc in center ch of next ch-5 lp—$5\frac{1}{2}$ ($6\frac{1}{2}$, $7\frac{1}{2}$, $8\frac{1}{2}$, $9\frac{1}{2}$) Mesh Sts.

Next Row (RS): Ch 1 and turn, work remaining 5 (6, 7, 8, 9) Mesh Sts.

Rep last 2 rows with one-half less Mesh St each row until 3 (4, 4, 5, 5) Mesh Sts rem.

Next Row: Work Row 2 of Mesh Pattern Flat—2 (3, 3, 4, 4) Mesh Sts with a Half-Mesh St at each end, fasten and end off.

Sleeves

Loosely ch 48 (52, 56, 60, 64). Begin Beaded Mesh Pattern in the Round—12 (13, 14, 15, 16) Mesh sts. [*Note:* Sizes M and 1X will have 2 consecutive Bsc at completion of Rnd 2. Keep alternating bead patt as for Body on subsequent rnds.]

Continue in Beaded Mesh Pattern in the Round until piece measures 18 (17, 16, 15, 14)" (45.5 [43, 40.5, 38, 35.5] cm) or 36 (34, 32, 30, 28) rnds total, ending with a WS beading row.

Shape Cap

Next Row (RS, dec row): Work Row 1 of Mesh Pattern Flat, working only first 10 (11, 12, 13, 14) Mesh Sts and ending with sc, then end with ch 2, dc in center ch of next ch-5 lp—11 (12, 13, 14, 15) Mesh Sts total.

Next Row (WS, dec row): Rep last row but work only first 9 (10, 11, 12, 13) Mesh Sts—10 (11, 12, 13, 14) Mesh Sts total.

Next Row (RS): Work row 2 of Mesh Pattern Flat—9 (10, 11, 12, 13) Mesh Sts with a Half-Mesh St at each end.

Next Row (WS): Work Row 1 of Mesh Pattern Flat, working only first 9 (10, 11, 12, 13) Mesh Sts and ending with sc, then end with ch 2, dc in center ch of next ch-5 lp—10 (11, 12, 13, 14) Mesh Sts total.

Next Row (RS, dec row): Work Row 1 of Mesh Pattern Flat and work only 9 (10, 11, 12, 13) Mesh Sts.

Next Row (WS): Work Row 2 of Mesh Pattern Flat—8 (9, 10, 11, 12) Mesh Sts with a Half-Mesh St at each end.

Next Row (RS): Work Row 1 of Mesh Pattern Flat,

working only first 8 (9, 10, 11, 12) Mesh Sts and ending with sc, then end with ch 2, dc in center ch of next ch-5 lp—9 (10, 11, 12, 13) Mesh Sts total.

Next Row (WS, dec row): Rep last row but work only first 7 (8, 9, 10, 11) Mesh Sts—8 (9, 10, 11, 12) Mesh Sts total.

For size S only:
Next Row (RS, dec row): Work Row 1 of Mesh Pattern Flat—7 Mesh Sts.

Next Row (WS): Work Row 2 of Mesh Pattern Flat—6 Mesh Sts with a Half-Mesh St at each end.

For all sizes:
Next Row (RS, dec row): Work Row 1 of Mesh Pattern Flat, working only first 6 (7, 8, 9, 10) Mesh Sts and ending with sc, then end with ch 2, dc in center ch of next ch-5 lp—7 (8, 9, 10, 11) Mesh Sts total.

Next Row (WS, dec row): Rep last row but work only first 5 (6, 7, 8, 9) Mesh Sts—6 (7, 8, 9, 10) Mesh Sts total.

Rep last 2 rows with 1 less Mesh St each row until 3 Mesh Sts rem. Fasten and end off.

Finishing
Block pieces to measurements. Sew shoulder seams. Set in sleeves.

Body Bottom Trim
Prestring 72 (80, 88, 96, 104) beads onto yarn. With WS facing, join to underside of beg foundation ch, ch 1, sc in same ch as join, *Bsc in underside of next ch, sc in underside of next ch; rep from * around, end Bsc in underside of last ch, join with sl st to first st. Fasten and end off.

Sleeve Bottom Trim
Prestring 24 (26, 28, 30, 32) beads onto yarn for each sleeve and work as for Body Bottom Trim.

Neck Trim
Prestring 36 (36, 45, 45, 54) beads onto yarn. With WS facing, evenly space 72 (72, 90, 90, 108, 108) sc around neck, working Bsc every other st. Fasten and end off.

Scallops and Some Half-Shells Bolero and Hat

Striping in the scallop stitch forms undulations, rather than straight horizontals. The shape of the stitch also lends itself to some natural shaping, for instance, in the underarms and sleeve caps. And buttonless openings mean not having to fiddle with buttonholes and buttonbands. Add the hat on page 133 in an unusual side-to-side construction that utilizes short rows.

Bolero

Finished Size

Sizes S (M, L, 1X, 2X, 3X): 37¼ (40, 42¾, 45½, 48, 50¾)" (94.5 [101.5, 108.5, 115, 122, 129] cm) bust/chest circumference. This is a loose-fitting garment. Sample was done in size M.

Materials

Yarn: Louet Sales Gems Merino Sport (100% merino wool, 225 yd [206 m]/100 g): burgundy (B), 4 (5, 6, 7, 8, 8) skeins and linen grey (G), 1 (1, 1, 2, 2, 2) skein(s).

Crochet hook: Size H/8 (5 mm). Adjust hook size if necessary to obtain the correct gauge.

Gauge

3 Shell Sts and 10 shell rows = 4" (10 cm).

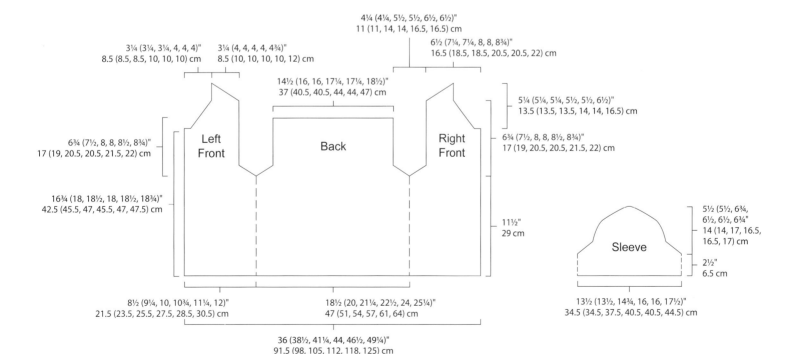

Notes
- Body is worked in one piece up to the underarms.
- Sleeves are worked circularly in rnds up to the cap.
- Front is slightly longer than Back to accommodate back-neck drop.

Special Stitches
Shell st: 5 dc in same st with a sc before and after this.

Stitch key
- ⌒ = chain (ch)
- + = single crochet (sc)
- ⊤ = double crochet (dc)
- ⋀ = Shell st (5 dc)

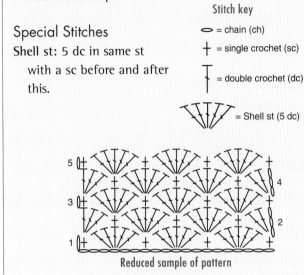

Reduced sample of pattern

Body

With B, loosely ch 164 (178, 188, 202, 212, 226).

For sizes S (L, 2X) only:

Row 1 (WS): Sc in 2nd ch from hook, *sk 2 ch, work 5 dc in next ch, sk 2 ch, sc in next ch; rep from * across—27 (31, 35) Shell Sts total.

Row 2 (RS): Ch 3 (counts as dc) and turn, work another 2 dc in first sc (half shell), *sk 2 dc, sc in next dc (the center dc of 5-dc shell), sk 2 dc, work 5 dc in next sc; rep from * across, end with only 3 dc in last sc (half shell)—26 (30, 34) full Shell Sts with a half-shell at each end.

Row 3 (WS): Ch 1 and turn, sc in first dc, *sk 2 dc, work 5 dc in next sc, sk 2 dc, sc in next dc (the center dc of 5-dc shell); rep from * across, end last sc in top of turning ch-3.

Rep Rows 2 and 3 for patt until 22 rows total have been completed, ending with Row 2 of patt and changing to G at last st.

*Work 2 rows in patt with G, change to B at last st *, work 2 rows in patt with B, change to G at last st, rep from * to *, end off G, work 2 rows in patt with B.

For sizes M (1X, 3X) only:

Row 1 (WS): 2 dc in 4th ch from hook, *sk 2 ch, sc in next ch, sk 2 ch, work 5 dc in next ch; rep from * across, ending with only 3 dc in last ch—28 (32, 36) full shell sts with a half-shell at each end.

Row 2 (RS): Ch 1 and turn, sc in first dc, *sk 2 dc, work 5 dc in next sc, sk 2 dc, sc in next dc (the center dc of 5-dc shell); rep from * across, end last sc in top of turning ch-3—29 (33, 37) Shell Sts total.

Row 3 (WS): Ch 3 (counts as dc) and turn, work another 2 dc in first sc, *sk 2 dc, sc in next dc (the center dc of 5-dc shell), sk 2 dc, work 5 dc in next sc; rep from * across, end with only 3 dc in last sc.

Rep Rows 2 and 3 for patt until 22 rows total have been completed, ending with Row 2 of patt and changing to G at last st.

*Work 2 rows in patt with G, change to B at last st *, work 2 rows in patt with B, change to G at last st, rep from * to *, end off G, work 2 rows in patt with B.

For all sizes:

Shape Left Front Armhole

Next Row (WS): Cont with B only and keeping to patt, work first 6 (6½, 7, 7½, 8, 8½) Shells only, ending with sc; do not work rem sts.

Next Row (RS): Turn, slip st into first sc and next 3 dc, ch 1, sc in same dc as last sl st (the center dc of 5-dc shell), cont row in est patt—5½ (6, 6½, 7, 7½, 8) shell sts total.

Next Row (WS): Keeping to patt, work first 5 (5½, 6, 6½, 7, 7½) shells only, ending with sc, do not work rem sts.

For sizes L (1X, 2X, 3X) only:

Next Row (RS): Turn, slip st into first sc and next 3 dc, ch 1, sc in same dc as last sl st (the center dc of 5-dc shell), cont row in est patt—5½ (6, 6½, 7) Shell Sts total.

For sizes 2X (3X) only:
Next Row (WS): Keeping to patt, work first 6 (6.5) shells only, ending with sc, do not work rem sts.

For all sizes:
Cont in patt on 5 (5.5, 5.5, 6, 6, 6.5) shells until piece measures $16\frac{3}{4}$ (18, $18\frac{1}{2}$, 18, $18\frac{1}{2}$, $18\frac{3}{4}$)" (42.5 [45.5, 47, 45.5, 47, 47.5] cm) total from beg or 42 (45, 46, 45, 46, 47) rows total have been completed.

Shape Neck

Keeping to patt, sk or sl st over two half-shells from neck edge as for armhole—4 (4.5, 4.5, 5, 5, 5.5) Shell Sts total.
Keeping to patt, sk or sl st over one half-shell from neck edge as for armhole—3.5 (4, 4, 4.5, 4.5, 5) Shell Sts total.
Keeping to patt, sk or sl st over one half-shell from neck edge as for armhole—3 (3.5, 3.5, 4, 4, 4.5) Shell Sts total.
Keeping to patt, sk or sl st over one half-shell from neck edge as for armhole—2.5 (3, 3, 3.5, 3.5, 4) Shell Sts total.

For sizes M (L, 1X, 2X, 3X) only:
Keeping to patt, sk or sl st over one half-shell from neck edge—2.5 (2.5, 3, 3, 3.5) Shell Sts total.

For size 3X only:
Keeping to patt, sk or sl st over one half-shell from neck edge—3 Shell Sts total.

For all sizes:
Work even in patt on 2.5 (2.5, 2.5, 3, 3, 3) shells until 51 (53, 54, 54, 55, 57) rows total have been worked.

Shape Shoulder

Keeping to patt, sk or sl st over one half-shell from armhole edge as for armhole—2 (2, 2, 2.5, 2.5, 2.5) Shell Sts total.
Keeping to patt, sk or sl st over one half-shell from armhole edge as for armhole—1.5 (1.5, 1.5, 2, 2, 2) Shell Sts total.
Keeping to patt, sk or sl st over one half-shell from armhole edge as for armhole—1 (1, 1, 1.5, 1.5, 1.5) Shell Sts total.

Keeping to patt, sk or sl st over one half-shell from armhole edge as for armhole—1/2 (1/2, 1/2, 1, 1, 1) Shell Sts total.

For sizes 1X (2X, 3X) only:
Keeping to patt, sk or sl st over one half-shell from armhole edge as for armhole —1/2 (1/2, 1/2) Shell Sts total.

For all sizes:
Fasten and end off, leaving 12" (30.5 cm) tail.

Shape Back Armholes
With WS facing, skip next two half-shell sts past first row of Left Front Armhole and join in next st, ch 1, sc in same st as join and cont to work 13 (14, 15, 16, 17, 18) Shell Sts total ending with sc.

Next Row (RS): Turn, slip st into first sc and next 3 dc, ch 1, sc in same dc as last sl st (the center dc of 5-dc shell), cont row in est patt, end with sc in center dc of last shell, do not work rem 2 dc and sc—12 (13, 14, 15, 16, 17) Shell Sts total.

Rep last row 1 (1, 2, 2, 3, 3) more times—11 (12, 12, 13, 13, 14) Shell Sts total.

Cont to work in patt with alt rows having 10 (11, 11, 12, 12, 13) shells with a half-shell at each end until piece measures 18 (18 3/4, 19 1/4, 19 1/4, 19 1/2, 20 1/2)" (45.5 [47.5, 49, 49, 49.5, 52] cm) total from beg or 45 (47, 48, 48, 49, 51) rows total have been worked. Fasten and end off.

Shape Right Front
With WS facing, skip next two half-shell sts past first row of Back and join in next st, ch 1, sc in same st as join and cont to work 6 (6 1/2, 7, 7 1/2, 8, 8 1/2) Shell Sts total. Work as for Left Front reversing all shaping.

Sleeves

With B, loosely ch 60 (60, 66, 72, 72, 78), join with sl st to first ch to form circle being careful not to twist.

Row 1 (WS): Ch 1, sc in same ch as joining sl st, *sk next 2 ch, 5-dc in next ch, sk next 2 ch, sc in next ch; rep from * ending without last sc but with sl st to first sc to join—10 (10, 11, 12, 12, 13) Shell Sts total.

Row 2 (RS): Ch 3 (counts as dc) and turn, dc in sl st at base of ch, *sk next 2 dc, sc in next dc, sk next 2 dc, 5-dc in next sc; rep from * ending with only 3 dc in sc at base of beg ch, join with sl st to top of beg ch-3 turning ch.

Row 3 (WS): Ch 1 and turn, sc in first dc, *sk next 2 dc, 5-dc in next sc, sk next 2 dc, sc in next dc; rep from * ending without last sc but with sl st to first sc to join.

Rep Rows 2 and 3 until 7 rows total have been worked.

Shape Cap

Dec Row: Turn, slip st into next 3 dc, ch 1, sc in same dc as last sl st, cont row in est patt, end with sc in center dc of last shell, do not work rem 2 dc and sc—9 (9, 10, 11, 11, 12) Shell Sts total.

Rep Dec Row 2 (2, 3, 3, 3, 3) times—7 (7, 7, 8, 8, 9) Shell Sts total.

Work 2 (2, 4, 2, 2, 2) rows even in patt.

Rep Dec Row once—6 (6, 6, 7, 7, 8) Shell Sts total.

Work 2 rows even in patt. Rep Dec Row until one shell remains. Fasten and end off.

Finishing

Block pieces to measurements. Sew Front shoulders to straight section of Back.
Set in sleeves.

Trim: With G, work 3 rows of sc evenly spaced around all edges, working extra sts at corners.

Hat

Finished Size
About 20" (50 cm) circumference at head opening and 8" (20 cm) long from top.

Materials
Yarn: Louet Sales Gems Opal Merino (100% merino wool: 225 yd [206 m]/100 g): burgundy (B) and grey linen (G), 1 skein each.

Crochet hooks: Size G/6 (4 mm). Adjust hook size if necessary to obtain the correct gauge.

Gauge
3 Shell sts and 10 rows = 4" (10 cm) in Shell St patt.

Notes

Top of hat is worked sideways using short rows to form wedges. Bottom trim is then picked up and worked in the round back and forth.

Special Stitches

Shell St: 5 dc in same st.

First Wedge

Row 1 (RS): With B, ch 32, sc in 2nd ch from hook, *sk 2 ch, 5 dc in next ch, sk 2 ch, sc in next ch; rep from * across—5 shells.

Row 2: Turn, sl st to center dc or 3rd dc of first shell, ch 1, sc in same dc as sl st, * sk next 2 dc, 5 dc in next sc, sk next 2 dc, sc in next dc; rep from * across, ending with only 3 dc in last sc—4 full shells with a half-shell at each end.

Row 3: Ch 1 and turn, sc in first dc, *sk next 2 dc, 5 dc in next sc, sk next 2 dc, sc in next dc; rep from * across, ending with only 4 full shells worked, do not work rem sts.

Row 4: Rep Row 2—3 full shells with a half-shell at end.

Row 5: Ch 1 and turn, sc in first dc, *sk next 2 dc, 5 dc in next sc, sk next 2 dc, sc in next dc; rep from * across, end with only 3 full shells worked, do not work rem sts.

Row 6: Rep Row 2—2 full shells with a half-shell at end, change to G at last st, end off B.

Second Wedge

Row 1: With G and RS facing, ch 1 and turn, sc in first dc, [sk next 2 dc, 5 dc in next sc, sk next 2 dc, sc in next dc] 2 times for 2 full shells worked, sk next 2 dc, sc in next row-end sc in row 5 of previous wedge, sk next 2 dc, 5 dc in next row-end sc in row 4 of previous wedge, sk next 2 dc, sc in next sc in row 3 of previous wedge, sk next 2 dc, 5 dc in next sc in row 2 of previous wedge, sk next 2 dc, sc in next sc in row 1 of previous wedge—5 full shells.

Rep Rows 2–6 of first wedge, change to B at last st, end off G.

Rep Second Wedge, alternating colors B and G until 10 wedges total have been completed, do not end off G. Clip yarn leaving 16" (41 cm) tail. Use tail to sew across top of last G wedge to beg foundation ch.

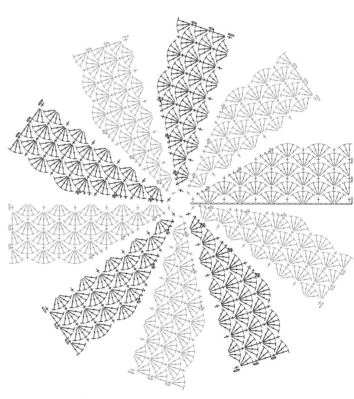

Ten pinwheel-type wedges are worked from side to side and shaped via short rows to form hat

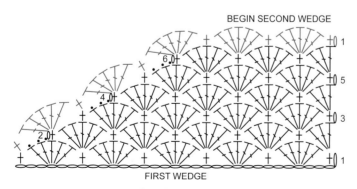

BEGIN SECOND WEDGE

FIRST WEDGE

Transition from first wedge to second wedge

Trim

With RS facing, join B to any sc at side edge of piece (which is bottom edge of hat).

Rnd 1: Ch 1, sc in same sc as join, *work 5 dc in next row-end sc along side edge of piece, work sc in next row-end sc along side edge of piece; rep from * around, join with sl st to first st—15 shells.

Rnd 2: Ch 3 and turn (counts as dc), work 2 more dc in first sc, sk next 2 dc, sc in next dc, sk next 2 dc, 5 dc in next sc; rep from * around, end with only 2 more dc in last sc, change to G at last st, join with sl st to top of beg ch-3, do not end off B.

Rnd 3: With G, ch 1 and turn, sc in first sc, *sk next 2 dc, 5 dc in next sc, sk next 2 dc, sc in next dc; rep from * around, end without last sc, change to B at last st, join with sl st to first sc, end off G.

Rnd 4: With B, rep rnd 2 but do not change to G.

Rnd 5: With B, rep rnd 3, fasten and end off.

TEN

Chevron-Stitch Construction

Also known as ripples, these classic patterns are a favorite for afghans. Applying shaping carves out curves for armholes, necklines, and the like. The basic principle is pretty straightforward: if you stack increases and decreases on top of one another, the increases form a hill and decreases form a valley.

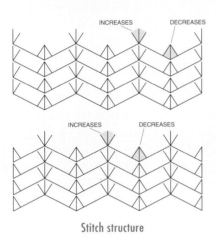

Stitch structure

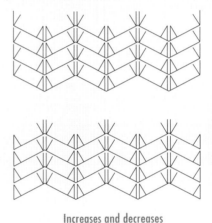

Increases and decreases

Notice how each increase is matched by a decrease and vice versa so that they cancel each other out and the stitch count across the row remains the same (above). Also note how, except for the side edges, the decreases and increases come in *pairs*, or double-decreases/double-increases (above right).

Double-increases and double-decreases need not be worked into just one stitch or become the same stitch. Instead, they can be worked side by side in pairs. When "spread out" like this, the peaks and valleys are less pointy and, instead, more rounded.

Frequently increasing and decreasing rows, like every single row or every other row, results in sharper angles in each chevron wedge (right).

Sharp angles with increases and decreases occurring often. The shorter the stitch height, the more angled the piece.

Subtle angles with increases and decreases occuring infrequently.
The taller the stitch height, the less angled the piece.

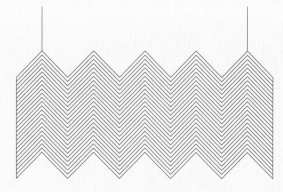

Built-in armhole shape

If the increasing and decreasing rows occur less frequently, like every third or fourth row, more subtle angles in each chevron wedge appear (above).

It will always take more stitches to get a certain width than if you were to do "straight" crocheting. That's due to the "bent lines." It is important to differentiate between this "angled" gauge versus a straight gauge. As mentioned in Chapter 5, think in terms of the width of each chevron wedge (or repeat), rather than actual gauge.

When going from the zigzags of a chevron piece to straight crocheting, "filling" in of the valleys or spaces is necessary. This can be done with shorter stitches, such as single crochet, at the peaks, then progressing to the longer stitches of half double and double crochet, culminating in longest treble crochets at the bottoms. *At the same time,* decreasing stitches is also necessary to narrow the straight crocheting portion. Remember: given the same number of stitches, straight pieces are wider than chevron fabrics. To figure out how many decreases are necessary, see how wide each chevron repeat is. Say it is 3 inches wide and is composed of 13 stitches. The regular "straight" gauge is necessary so do a swatch. It may measure 3 stitches per inch. That means 3 inches straight across is made up of only 9 stitches, so the 13 stitches of the chevron have to decrease by 4 stitches in order to get 9 instead. Thus, working differing stitch heights while decreasing might look something like the illustration at the left.

Filling in the valley
of a chevron

Notice that if it begins with an "up," it ends with a "down," and vice versa, as in the illustrations on page 137. The desired overall shape will determine which you choose. For instance, note how an armhole is "built-in" when using the "begin with up, end with down" chevrons (above). This is how I worked the armholes in my Flying Trapeze Tunic.

For V necks, it's only logical to think of the valley of a chevron at dead-center. Hence, the use of a single chevron shape in my striped Chic Chevron Pullover. A peak, though, forms the halter shape in the wedding gown. If all the points at the top of a piece are gathered together and the sides of each peak are sewn together, wedges like a pizza pie form a circle. This is how the top of the Flying Trapeze Hat is closed.

For overall shaping within the fabric, alter the number (and therefore the width) of any given chevron repeat. This is achieved in two ways. An extra stitch can always be inserted into the plain areas between each increase/decrease point, or a stitch can be taken away in this same area. Here's a more invisible, refined way: when a decrease or increase is *not* compensated for, the net will be a *real* increase or decrease! So if the decreases are worked across the row but the accompanying increases are not, there will be a narrowing of the whole piece and each chevron repeat will have two less stitches. This is how the Flying Trapeze Tunic's body is shaped (opposite, top).

Conversely, if the increases are worked across the row but the accompanying decreases are not, there will be a widening of the whole piece and each chevron repeat will have two more stitches. The Flying Trapeze Tunic's collar is shaped in this manner.

If narrowing or widening all the repeats results in too much radical shaping, then just do shaping in one or a few chevrons, not all of them. In the swatch shown

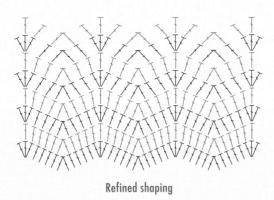

Refined shaping

Swatch of single decreasing chevron

here, a single chevron repeat "disappears" as it decreases away, leaving the other chevrons intact. This would be ideal for vertical dart shaping.

The Altar Halter is nothing but one giant, single chevron. Since the number of stitches between the increase and decrease points is large, I shaped for the waist as I would normally for any side shaping in a "straight" piece. The chevron structure offers such sculptural possibilities, and I'm not even close to depleting its uses and manipulations. So many things to design, so little time . . .

Flying Trapeze Tunic and Hat

Reminiscent of the house of Missoni, the three-colored stripes accentuate the
undulating movement of the fabric. The trapeze, or tent, shape is very forgiving
for all figure types. The matching hat is easily shaped by sewing together
the sides of each chevron wedge at the top.

Tunic

Finished Size

S (M, L, 1X, 2X, 3X): 36½ (40, 44, 48, 52, 56)" (92.5
[101.5, 112, 122, 132, 142] cm) bust/chest circumference.
This is a loose-fitting garment. Sample was done in size M.

Materials

Yarn: Brown Sheep Nature Spun Sport (100% wool,
184 yd [169 m]/50 g): #110 blueberry (Bl), #308
sunburst gold (G), #N94 Bev's bear (Br), 4 (4, 4, 5,
5, 6) skeins each.

Crochet hook: Size G/6 (4 mm). Adjust hook size if
necessary to obtain the correct gauge.

Notions: Smooth, contrast-color yarn to use as markers
(optional).

Gauge

Steam-block and hang swatches before
measuring gauge.

16 sts = 4" (10 cm) in dc.

8 dc rows in all chevron patts = 4"
(10 cm), measured straight up line of
inc's or dec's.

One 20-st chevron rep (8 sts between
inc/dec's) = 4⅛" (10.625 cm).

One 18-st chevron rep (7 sts between
inc/dec's) = 3¾" (9.375 cm).

One 16-st chevron rep (6 sts between
inc/dec's) = 3½" (8.75 cm).

One 14-st chevron rep (5 sts between inc/dec's) = 3"
(7.5 cm).

One 12-st chevron rep (4 sts between inc/dec's) = 2½"
(6.25 cm).

One 10-st chevron rep (3 sts between inc/dec's) = 2¼"
(5.625 cm).

One 8-st chevron rep (2 sts between inc/dec's) = 1¾"
(4.375 cm).

One 6-st chevron rep (1 st between inc/dec's) = 1½"
(3.75 cm).

One 4-st chevron rep (0 sts between inc/dec's) = 1" (2.5 cm).

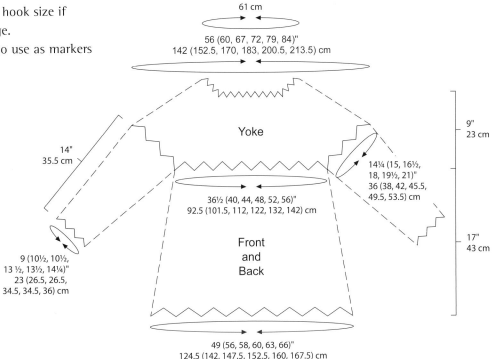

24"
61 cm

56 (60, 67, 72, 79, 84)"
142 (152.5, 170, 183, 200.5, 213.5) cm

14"
35.5 cm

Yoke

9"
23 cm

14¼ (15, 16½,
18, 19½, 21)"
36 (38, 42, 45.5,
49.5, 53.5) cm

36½ (40, 44, 48, 52, 56)"
92.5 (101.5, 112, 122, 132, 142) cm

9 (10½, 10½,
13 ½, 13½, 14¼)"
23 (26.5, 26.5,
34.5, 34.5, 36) cm

Front
and
Back

17"
43 cm

49 (56, 58, 60, 63, 66)"
124.5 (142, 147.5, 152.5, 160, 167.5) cm

Notes

- Tunic is worked from bottom up in the round. Sleeves are worked separately, then joined with body at the yoke.
- Carry colors not in use loosely on WS. In particular, be sure to carry colors not in use on OUTSIDE of cowl collar so carries aren't visible when collar is flipped down and worn.

Stripe Sequence

For Body: [3 rnds Bl, 2 rnds Br, 1 rnd G] 3 times, [2 rnds Bl, 2 rnds Br, 2 rnds G] 3 times, [1 rnd Bl, 2 rnds Br, 3 rnds G] 4 times, [2 rnds Br, 1 rnd Bl, 3 rnds G] once.

For Sleeve: [3 rnds Bl, 2 rnds Br, 1 rnd G] 2 times, [2 rnds Bl, 2 rnds Br, 2 rnds G] 2 times, [2 rnds Bl, 2 rnds Br] once before Sleeve is joined to Body, then follow remainder of Body sequence.

Special Stitches

Dec: Yarn around hook and pick up lp in next st, yarn around hook and pull through 2 lps on hook, twice, yarn around hook and pull through rem 3 lps on hook.

Double-dec: Yarn around hook and pick up lp in next st, yarn around hook and pull through 2 lps on hook, sk next st, yarn around hook and pick up lp in next st, yarn around hook and pull through 2 lps on hook, yarn around hook and pull through rem 3 lps on hook.

Inc: Work 2 dc all in same st.

Double-inc: Work 3 dc all in same st.

Quadruple inc: Work 5 dc all in same st.

20-st chevron rep (8 sts between inc/dec's): *Dc in each of next 8 sts, double-dec next 3 sts tog, dc in each of next 8 sts, work 3 dc in next st; rep from *.

18-st chevron rep (7 sts between inc/dec's): *Dc in each of next 7 sts, double-dec next 3 sts tog, dc in each of next 7 sts, work 3 dc in next st; rep from *.

16-st chevron rep (6 sts between inc/dec's): *Dc in each of next 6 sts, double-dec next 3 sts tog, dc in each of next 6 sts, work 3 dc in next st; rep from *.

14-st chevron rep (5 sts between inc/dec's): *Dc in each of next 5 sts, double-dec next 3 sts tog, dc in each of next 5 sts, work 3 dc in next st; rep from *.

12-st chevron rep (4 sts between inc/dec's): *Dc in each of next 4 sts, double-dec next 3 sts tog, dc in each of next 4 sts, work 3 dc in next st; rep from *.

10-st chevron rep (3 sts between inc/dec's): *Dc in each of next 3 sts, double-dec next 3 sts tog, dc in each of next 3 sts, work 3 dc in next st; rep from *.

8-st chevron rep (2 sts between inc/dec's): *Dc in each of next 2 sts, double-dec next 3 sts tog, dc in each of next 2 sts, work 3 dc in next st; rep from *.

6-st chevron rep (1 st between inc/dec's): *Dc in next st, double-dec next 3 sts tog, dc in next st, work 3 dc in next st; rep from *.

4-st chevron rep (0 sts between inc/dec's): *Double-dec next 3 sts tog, work 3 dc in next st; rep from *.

See stitch diagrams.

Chevron hat

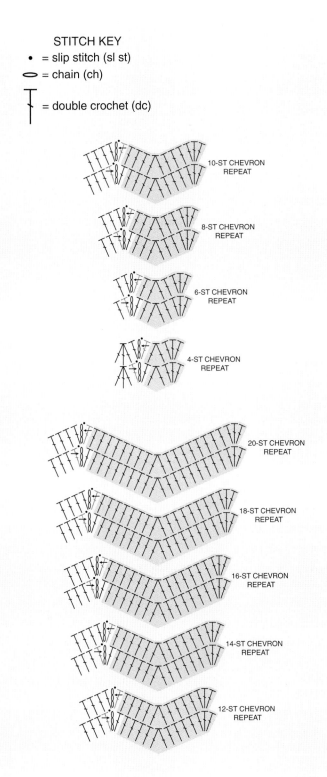

STITCH KEY

- • = slip stitch (sl st)
- ◠ = chain (ch)
- ⊤ = double crochet (dc)

10-ST CHEVRON
REPEAT

8-ST CHEVRON
REPEAT

6-ST CHEVRON
REPEAT

4-ST CHEVRON
REPEAT

20-ST CHEVRON
REPEAT

18-ST CHEVRON
REPEAT

16-ST CHEVRON
REPEAT

14-ST CHEVRON
REPEAT

12-ST CHEVRON
REPEAT

Body

With Bl, loosely ch 228 (256, 272, 288, 304, 320). Join with sl st to first ch, being careful not to twist.

For size S only, Rnd 1 (WS): Ch 3 (counts as dc), work another dc in base of ch, *dc in each of next 5 ch, work double-dec over next 3 ch, dc in each of next 5 ch **, 3 dc in next ch *, work from * to * a total of 4 times, + dc in each of next 6 ch, work double-dec over next 3 ch, dc in each of next 6 ch, 3 dc in next ch +, rep from * to * 7 times, rep from ** to ** once, rep from * to * 3 times, end last rep at **, work one more dc at base of beg ch, join with sl st to top of beg ch.

For sizes M (L, 1X, 2X, 3X), Rnd 1 (WS): Ch 3 (counts as dc), work another dc in base of ch, *dc in each of next 6 (7, 7, 8, 8) ch, work double-dec over next 3 ch, dc in each of next 6 (7, 7, 8, 8) ch, 3 dc in next ch, dc in each of next 6 (6, 7, 7, 8) ch, work double-dec over next 3 ch, dc in each of next 6 (6, 7, 7, 8) ch, **3 dc in next ch *, rep from * to * across, end last rep at +, work one more dc at base of beg ch, join with sl st to top of beg ch.

Rnd 2: Ch 3 and turn (counts as dc), work another dc in base of ch, work in est chevron patt as foll:

Size S: 4 [14-st] chevrons, 1 [16-st] chevron, 7 [14-st] chevrons, 1 [16-st] chevron, and 3 [14-st] chevrons.

Size M: 16 [16-st] chevrons.

Size L: Alternating [18-st] chevrons with [16-st] chevrons 8 times.

Size 1X: 16 [18-st] chevrons.

Size 2X: Alternating [20-st] chevrons with [18-st] chevrons 8 times.

Size 3X: 16 [20-st] chevrons.

Note that all double-inc's fall on top of one another and all double-dec's fall on top of one another as a way to keep track. You may also use contrasting colored yarn as markers or aids to keep track of different-size chevron repeats.

Cont to work in est chevron patts in stripe sequence until 11 rnds total have been completed.

Rnd 12: Cont in stripe sequence and dec in each section of dc between each double-inc/double-dec pair and each double-dec/double-inc pair—32 sts dec'd, 196 (224, 240, 256, 272, 288) sts rem.

Rnd 13: Ch 3 and turn (counts as dc), work another dc in base of ch, work in est chevron patt as foll:

Size S: 4 [12-st] chevrons, 1 [14-st] chevron, 7 [12-st] chevrons, 1 [14-st] chevron, and 3 [12-st] chevrons.

Size M: 16 [14-st] chevrons.

Size L: Alternating [16-st] chevrons with [14-st] chevrons.

Size 1X: 16 [16-st] chevrons.

Size 2X: Alternating [18-st] chevrons with [16-st] chevrons.

Size 3X: 16 [18-st] chevrons.

Cont to work in est chevron patts in stripe sequence until 23 rnds total have been completed.

Rnd 24: Cont in stripe sequence and dec in each section of dc between each double-inc/double-dec pair and each double-dec/double-inc pair—32 sts dec'd, 164 (192, 208, 224, 240, 256) sts rem.

Rnd 25: Ch 3 and turn (counts as dc), work another dc in base of ch, work in est chevron patt as foll:

Size S: 4 [10-st] chevrons, 1 [12-st] chevron, 7 [10-st] chevrons, 1 [12-st] chevron, and 3 [10-st] chevrons.

Size M: 16 [12-st] chevrons.

Size L: Alternating [14-st] chevrons with [12-st] chevrons.

Size 1X: 16 [14-st] chevrons.

Size 2X: Alternating [16-st] chevrons with [14-st] chevrons.

Size 3X: 16 [16-st] chevrons.

Cont to work in est chevron patts in stripe sequence until 34 rnds total have been completed. Set work aside to be completed with Sleeves.

Sleeves

With Bl, loosely ch 36 (48, 48, 60, 60, 66), join with sl st to first ch being careful not to twist.

Rnd 1 (WS): Ch 3 (counts as dc), work another dc in base of ch, *dc in each of next 1 (2, 2, 3, 3, 4) ch, work double-dec over next 3 ch, dc in each of next 1 (2, 2, 3, 3, 4) ch, 3 dc in next ch, dc in each of next 1 (2, 2, 3, 3, 3) ch, work double-dec over next 3 ch, dc in each of next 1 (2, 2, 3, 3, 3) ch, **3 dc in next ch *; rep from * to * across, end last rep at **, work one more dc at base of beg ch, join with sl st to top of beg ch.

Rnd 2: Ch 3 and turn (counts as dc), work another dc in base of ch, work in est chevron patt as foll:

Size S: 6 [6-st] chevrons.

Sizes M (L): 6 [8-st] chevrons.

Sizes 1X (2X): 6 [10-st] chevrons.

Size 3X: Alternating [12-st] chevrons with [10-st] chevrons 3 times.

Note that all double-inc's fall on top of one another and all double-dec's fall on top of one another as a way to keep track.

Cont to work in est chevron patts in stripe sequence until 7 rnds total have been completed.

Rnd 8: Cont in stripe sequence but work quadruple inc or 5 dc in same st instead of double-inc of 3 dc in same st—48 (60, 60, 72, 72, 78) sts.

Rnd 9: Ch 3 and turn (counts as dc), work another dc in base of ch, work in est chevron patt as foll:

Size S: 6 [8-st] chevrons.

Sizes M (L): 6 [10-st] chevrons.

Sizes 1X (2X): 6 [12-st] chevrons.

Size 3X: Alternating [14-st] chevrons with [12-st] chevrons 3 times.

Cont to work in est chevron patts in stripe sequence until 13 rnds total have been completed.

Rnd 14: Cont in stripe sequence and inc in each section of dc between each double-inc/double-dec pair and each double-dec/double-inc pair—60 (72, 72, 84, 84, 90) sts.

Rnd 15: Ch 3 and turn (counts as dc), work another dc in base of ch, work in est chevron patt as foll:

Size S: 6 [10-st] chevrons.

Sizes M (L): 6 [12-st] chevrons.

Sizes 1X (2X): 6 [14-st] chevrons.

Size 3X: Alternating [16-st] chevrons with [14-st] chevrons 3 times.

Cont to work in est chevron patts in stripe sequence until 19 rnds total have been completed.

Rnd 20: Cont in stripe sequence and inc to 66 (72, 78, 84, 90, 96) sts as foll:

Size S: Inc each dc section of next [10-st] chevron and every alternate [10-st] chevron.

Size M: Do not inc.

Size L: Inc each dc section of next [12-st] chevron and every alternate [12-st] chevron.

Size 1X: Do not inc.

Size 2X: Inc each dc section of next [14-st] chevron and every [14-st] chevron.

Size 3X: Inc each dc section of each [14-st] chevron.

Rnd 21: Ch 3 and turn (counts as dc), work another dc in base of ch, work in est chevron patt as foll:

Size S: Alternating [12-st] chevrons with [10-st] chevrons 3 times.

Size M: 6 [12-st] chevrons.

Size L: Alternating [14-st] chevrons with [12-st] chevrons 3 times.

Size 1X: 6 [14-st] chevrons.

Size 2X: Alternating [16-st] chevrons with [14-st] chevrons 3 times.

Size 3X: 6 [16-st] chevrons.

Cont to work in est chevron patts in stripe sequence until 28 rnds total have been completed. Fasten and end off.

Yoke

Joining Rnd/Rnd 35 of Body/Rnd 29 of Sleeve (WS):
Picking up yarn from where Body was left off, ch 3 and turn so that WS faces, *work in est chevron patts in stripe sequence across next 7 chevron repeats ending right before increase, work dc in center dc of previous inc, have WS of Sleeve facing, yo hook, insert hook into same dc as well as into top of ch-3 of last row of Sleeve, yo hook and pick up lp joining the 2 pieces, complete dc, dc in top of ch-3 of last row of Sleeve, work in est chevron patts in stripe

sequence across next 5 chevron repeats of joined Sleeve ending right before increase *, work dc in center dc of previous inc, yo hook, insert hook into same dc, skip full rep of next Body Chevron and insert hook into center dc of previous inc of Body, yo hook and pick up lp joining the 2 pieces again, complete dc, dc in same joined-dc of Body; rep from * to * with other Sleeve, yo hook, insert hook into dc of inc, skip full rep of next Body Chevron and insert hook into center base of ch-3 at beg of rnd, yo hook and pick up lp joining the 2 pieces again, complete dc, join with sl st to top of beg ch-3—256 (288, 316, 336, 364, 384) sts made up of 24 chevrons of varying sizes around thus:

Size S: 3 [10-st] chevrons, 1 [12-st] chevron, 3 [10-st] chevrons for each Body, [12-st] chevron alternating with [10-st] chevron for five chevrons each Sleeve.

Size M: 7 [12-st] chevrons for each Body and 5 [12-st] chevrons for each Sleeve.

Size L: [14-st] chevron alternating with [12-st] chevron for 7 chevrons each Body, [14-st] chevron alternating with [12-st] chevron for 5 chevrons each Sleeve.

Size 1X: 7 [14-st] chevrons for each Body and 5 [14-st] chevrons for each Sleeve.

Size 2X: [16-st] chevron alternating with [14-st] chevron for seven chevrons each Body, [16-st] chevron alternating with [14-st] chevron for five chevrons each Sleeve.

Size 3X: 7 [16-st] chevrons for each Body and 5 [16-st] chevrons for each Sleeve.

Rnd 36 of Body (RS): Cont in stripe sequence and dec in each section of dc between each double-inc/double-dec pair and each double-dec/double-inc pair—208 (240, 268, 288, 316, 336) sts or work as foll:

Size S: 3 [8-st] chevrons, 1 [10-st] chevron, 3 [8-st] chevrons for each Body, [10-st] chevron alternating with [8-st] chevron for five chevrons each Sleeve.

Size M: 7 [10-st] chevrons for each Body and 5 [10-st] chevrons for each Sleeve.

Size L: [12-st] chevron alternating with [10-st] chevron for 7 chevrons each Body, [12-st] chevron alternating with [10-st] chevron for 5 chevrons each Sleeve.

Size 1X: 7 [12-st] chevrons for each Body and 5 [12-st] chevrons for each Sleeve.

Size 2X: [14-st] chevron alternating with [12-st] chevron

for 7 chevrons each Body, [14-st] chevron alternating with [12-st] chevron for 5 chevrons each Sleeve.

Size 3X: 7 [14-st] chevrons for each Body and 5 [14-st] chevrons for each Sleeve.

Cont to work in est chevron patts in stripe sequence until 37 rnds total have been completed.

For sizes L (2X) only, Rnd 38: Dec in each dc section of 12 (14) st chevron only to create all 10 (12) st chevrons—240 (288) sts.

Cont to work in est chevron patts in stripe sequence until 41 rnds total have been completed.

Rnd 42: Cont in stripe sequence and dec in each section of dc between each double-inc/double-dec pair and each double-dec/double-inc pair—160 (192, 192, 240, 240, 288) sts or work as foll:

Size S: 3 [6-st] chevrons, 1 [8-st] chevron, 3 [6-st] chevrons for each Body, [8-st] chevron alternating with [6-st] chevron for 5 chevrons each Sleeve.

Sizes M (L): 7 [8-st] chevrons for each Body and 5 [8-st] chevrons for each Sleeve.

Sizes 1X (2X): 7 [10-st] chevrons for each Body and 5 [10-st] chevrons for each Sleeve.

Size 3X: 7 [12-st] chevrons for each Body and 5 [12-st] chevrons for each Sleeve.

For size 3X only, Rnd 43: Cont in stripe sequence and dec in each section of dc between each double-inc/double-dec pair and each double-dec/double-inc pair—240 sts or 7 [10-st] chevrons for each Body and 5 [10-st] chevrons for each Sleeve.

Cont to work in est chevron patts in stripe sequence until 45 rnds total have been completed.

Rnd 46: Cont in stripe sequence and dec in each section of dc between each double-inc/double-dec pair and each double-dec/double-inc pair (for size S this means skip the dc between them altogether in the 6-st chevrons)—112 (144, 144, 192, 192, 192) sts or work as foll:

Size S: 3 [4-st] chevrons, 1 [6-st] chevron, 3 [4-st] chevrons for each Body, [6-st] chevron alternating with [4-st] chevron for 5 chevrons each Sleeve.

Sizes M (L): 7 [6-st] chevrons for each Body and 5 [6-st] chevrons for each Sleeve.

Sizes 1X (2X, 3X): 7 [8-st] chevrons for each Body and 5 [8-st] chevrons for each Sleeve.

For sizes 1X (2X, 3X) only, Rnd 47: Cont in stripe sequence and dec in each section of dc between each double-inc/double-dec pair and each double-dec/double-inc pair—144 sts or 7 [6-st] chevrons for each Body and 5 [6-st] chevrons for each Sleeve.

Cont to work in established chevron patts in stripe sequence until 49 rnds total have been completed.

For size S only, Rnd 50: Dec in each dc section of [6-st] chevrons only to create all [4-st] chevrons by skipping the dc between them altogether—96 sts.

For sizes M (L, 1X, 2X, 3X), Rnd 50: Cont in stripe sequence and dec in each section of dc between each double-inc/double-dec pair and each double-dec/double-inc pair (this means skip the dc between them altogether)—96 sts.

Cont to work 7 [4-st] chevrons for each Body and 5 [4-st] chevrons for each Sleeve in stripe sequence until 57 rnds total have been completed.

Cowl Collar

Rnd 58: Cont in stripe sequence and work quadruple-inc or 5-dc in same st instead of double-inc's—144 sts or 24 [6-st] chevrons total.

Cont to work in est chevron patts in stripe sequence until 61 rnds total have been completed.

Rnd 62: Cont in stripe sequence and work quadruple-inc or 5-dc in same st instead of double-inc's—192 sts or 24 [8-st] chevrons total.

Cont to work in est chevron patts in stripe sequence until 66 Body rnds total have been completed. Fasten and end off.

Finishing

Steam-block to measurements and to smooth out increases and decreases.

Hat

Finished Size
About 22½" (57 cm) around in circumference at head opening and 10" (25.5 cm) long from top.

Materials
Yarn: Brown Sheep Nature Spun Sport (100% wool, 184 yd [169 m]/50 g): #110 blueberry (Bl), #308 sunburst gold (G), #N94 Bev's bear (Br), 1 skein each.

Crochet hook: Size H/8 (5 mm). Adjust hook size if necessary to obtain the correct gauge.

Gauge
One 16-st chevron repeat = 3¾" (9.5 cm).

Notes
• Hat is worked from top down. Carry colors not in use loosely on WS.

Starting at top of hat, with G, make slipknot leaving an 18" (45.5 cm) tail, loosely ch 96, join with sl st to first ch being careful not to twist ch.

Rnd 1 (WS): Ch 3 (counts as dc), work another dc in base of ch, *dc in each of next 6 ch, [yarn around hook and pick up lp in next ch, yarn around hook and pull through 2 lps on hook, sk next ch, yarn around hook and pick up lp in next ch, yarn around hook and pull through 2 lps on hook, yarn around hook and pull through rem 3 lps on hook] for double-dec, dc in each of next 6 ch**, 3 dc in next ch; rep from * across, ending last rep at **, work 1 more dc at base of beg ch and change to Br at last st, join with sl st to top of beg ch.

Rnd 2: With Br, ch 3 and turn (counts as dc), work another dc in base of ch, *dc in each of next 6 dc, [yarn around hook and pick up lp in next dc, yarn around hook and pull through 2 lps on hook, sk next dc, yarn around hook and pick up lp in next dc, yarn around hook and pull through 2 lps on hook, yarn around hook and pull through rem 3 lps on hook] for double-dec, dc in each of next 6 dc**, 3 dc in next dc; rep from * across, ending last rep at **, work 1 more dc at base of beg ch and change to Bl at last st, join with sl st to top of beg ch.

Rnd 3: With Bl, rep Rnd 2 and change to G at last st.

Rnd 4: With G, rep Rnd 2 and change to Br at last st.

Rep Rnds 2–4 until 19 rows have been completed, fasten and end off.

Finishing
With long tail at beg, sew sides of each chevron tog as per diagram.

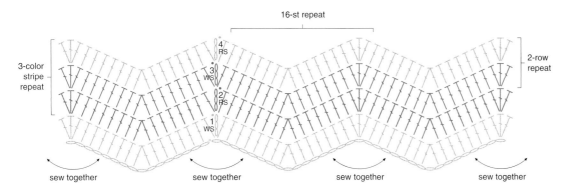

Chic Chevron Pullover

The use of Tunisian or Afghan crochet techniques make for a nice, drapey fabric
that is neither stiff nor bulky. Because loops are collected on a long and/or flexible
hook and worked off two at a time, it emulates knitting more than usual crochet.
The standard technique of working the regular Afghan stitch can be found in
a good reference book. My own take on the Tunisian purl stitch deviates from
the norm, however. Be sure to review the special stitches section on page 150.

Finished Size
36 (39½, 41½, 44½, 46½, 49½)" (91.5 [100.5, 105.5,
113, 118, 125.5] cm) bust/chest circumference. This is
a standard-fitting garment. Pullover shown measures
39½" (100.5 cm).

Materials
Yarn: Mission Falls 1824 (100% merino superwash wool,
   85 yd [78 m]/50 g): #09 nectar (N), 8 (8, 9, 10, 11,
   12) skeins; #08 earth (E), 4 (4, 5, 6, 6, 7) balls.
Crochet hook: Tunisian or Afghan hook size K/10½
   (6.5 mm). Size H/8 (5 mm) regular hook for trim.

Adjust hook size if necessary to obtain the correct
   gauge.
Notions: Smooth, contrast-color yarn to act as markers.
Gauge
13 sts and 10 rows = 4" (10 cm) in regular Tunisian st.

Notes
Center back and front panels are worked first, each from
the bottom up in a chevron pattern. Stitches are picked up
for the side panels from the center panels, and worked
outwards to the cuffs.

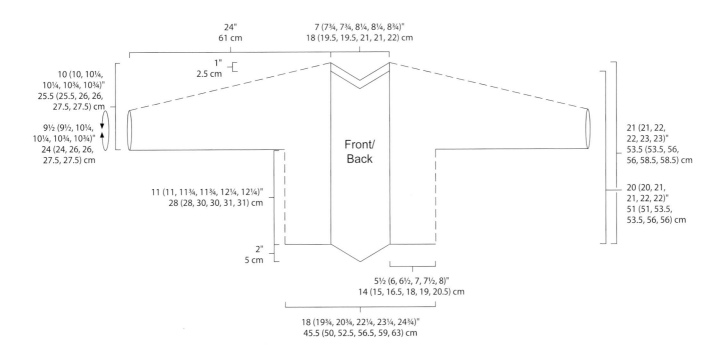

24"
61 cm

7 (7¾, 7¾, 8¼, 8¼, 8¾)"
18 (19.5, 19.5, 21, 21, 22) cm

1"
2.5 cm

10 (10, 10¼,
10¼, 10¾, 10¾)"
25.5 (25.5, 26, 26,
27.5, 27.5) cm

9½ (9½, 10¼,
10¼, 10¾, 10¾)"
24 (24, 26, 26,
27.5, 27.5) cm

Front/
Back

21 (21, 22,
22, 23, 23)"
53.5 (53.5, 56,
56, 58.5, 58.5) cm

11 (11, 11¾, 11¾, 12¼, 12¼)"
28 (28, 30, 30, 31, 31) cm

20 (20, 21,
21, 22, 22)"
51 (51, 53.5,
53.5, 56, 56) cm

2"
5 cm

5½ (6, 6½, 7, 7½, 8)"
14 (15, 16.5, 18, 19, 20.5) cm

18 (19¾, 20¾, 22¼, 23¼, 24¾)"
45.5 (50, 52.5, 56.5, 59, 63) cm

149

Special Stitches

Tunisian st (worked in 2 parts per row, RS always faces):

First part of row: Working from right to left, pick up loops as follows: sk first ch, *insert hook under front vertical bar of next st, yo and pull through vertical bar, rep from * to last st, insert hook under 2 strands of last ch, yo and pull through both strands.

Second part of row: Working from left to right, work off loops as follows: yo and pull through one loop for last ch, *yo and pull through 2 loops, rep from * across.

Tunisian Purl st (worked in 2 parts per row, RS always faces):

First part of row: Working from right to left, pick up loops as follows: sk first ch, *insert hook under back vertical bar behind next st, yo and pull through vertical bar, rep from * to last st, insert hook under 2 strands of last ch, yo and pull through both strands.

Second part of row: Working from left to right, work off loops as follows: yo and pull through one loop for last ch, *yo and pull through 2 loops, rep from * across.

To inc in Tunisian st, insert hook under horizontal bar between 2 vertical bars, then yo and pull through horizontal bar.

To dec in Tunisian st, insert hook under 2 consecutive vertical bars, then yo and pull through both vertical bars.

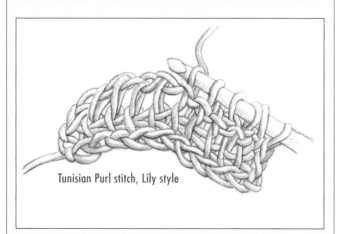

Tunisian Purl stitch, Lily style

Stripe Sequences

For Center V-Panel

Row 1: With E, pick up and work in Tunisian Purl, work off lps and change to N at last st at right side or when working off last 2 lps.

Row 2: With N, work in Tunisian St and change to E at last st at right side or when working off last 2 lps.

Rep Rows 1 and 2 for patt.

For Side Panels

Row 1: With N, work in Tunisian St.

Row 2: With N, work in Tunisian Purl.

Row 3: With N, pick up in Tunisian St for first part of row and change to E at left side, work second part of row with E.

Row 4: With E, work in Tunisian St.

Row 5: With E, pick up in Tunisian Purl for first part of row and change to N at left side, work second part of row with N.

Row 6: With N, work in Tunisian St.

Rep Rows 1–6 for patt.

Body

Back Center V-Panel

With N, loosely ch 28 (30, 30, 32, 32, 34). *Note:* St count remains constant throughout.

Row 1: Work in Tunisian St, picking up lp in 2nd ch from hook and in each ch across and changing to E at last st at right side.

Begin working Stripe Sequence for Center V-Panel.

Next Row: Cont Stripe Sequence for Center V-Panel but after picking up first lp, work inc, *pick up in next 10 (11, 11, 12, 12, 13) sts *, [work dec] twice, rep from * to *, work inc, pick up in next lp, then pick up in last ch, work off lps.

Next Row: Cont Stripe Sequence for Center V-Panel. Rep last 2 rows until side edge of piece measures 21 (21, 22, 22, 23, 23)" (53.5 [53.5, 56, 56, 58.5, 58.5] cm). Sl st across all lps either in front or in back according to patt; ch 3 at end. Fasten and end off, leaving 4" (10 cm) tail.

Front Center V-Panel

Work as for Back Center V-Panel for 20 (20, 21, 21, 22, 22)" (51 [51, 53.5, 53.5, 56, 56] cm) only.

Left Side Panel

Position both Center V-Panels in front of you with RS facing, Front panel on the right, and Back panel on the left. Attach ch 3s at ends to other side panel to link Center Panels at Neck and to give depth to Front Neck. With N, pick up 65 (65, 68, 68, 71, 71) lps evenly spaced along edge of Front Center panel, pick up a lp in each of 3 chs for neck opening, pick up 69 (69, 72, 72, 75, 75) sts evenly spaced along edge of Back Center panel—137 (137, 143, 143, 149, 149) lps total. Work off lps, marking 69th (69th, 72nd, 72nd, 75th, 75th) lp with contrast-color yarn as center st.

Begin working Stripe Sequence for Side Panel.

Shape Shoulders

Next Row: Keeping in est patt, work to within 2 sts of center, work dec, pick up lp in center st, work dec, complete row—135 (135, 141, 141, 147, 147) lps total.

Work this dec row every 3rd row a total of 12 times, then every 4th row 5 times.

Shape Sides

AT THE SAME TIME, when Side Panel measures 5½ (6, 6½, 7, 7½, 8)" (14 [15, 16.5, 18, 19, 20.5] cm) from beg, sl st in patt across first 36 (36, 38, 38, 40, 40) lps, work to within last 36 (36, 38, 38, 40, 40) lps, join another strand of yarn and sl st in patt across these last rem sts, fasten and end off.

Cont on rem sts in patt until Side Panel measures 24" (61 cm) from beg, sl st in patt across rem 31 (31, 33, 33, 35, 35) sts, fasten and end off.

Right Side Panel

Position both Center V-Panels in front of you with RS facing, Back panel on the right, and Front panel on the left. With N, pick up 69 (69, 72, 72, 75, 75) sts evenly spaced along edge of Back Center panel, pick up a lp in each of 3 chs for neck opening, pick up 65 (65, 68, 68, 71, 71) lps evenly spaced along edge of Front Center panel—137 (137, 143, 143, 149, 149) lps total. Work off lps, marking 69th (69th, 72nd, 72nd, 75th, 75th) lp with contrast-color yarn as center st.

Complete as for Left Side Panel.

Finishing

Block to measurements. Sew side and sleeve seams. With RS facing, N, and regular hook, work sc evenly around

Altar Halter and Let Your Fingers Do the Walking Gloves

One giant chevron is all that this top is made of, as are the gloves. The self-shaping creates the overall form. Subtle yarn textures in the same hue draw attention to the chevron lines, and shaping at the sides enhances the overall silhouette.

Finished Size

30 (32, 34, 36, 38, 40)" (76 [81.5, 86.5, 91.5, 96.5, 101.5] cm) bust/chest circumference. This is a close-fitting garment. Sample shown measures 32" (81.5 cm).

Materials

Yarn: Lily Chin Signature Collection Greenwich Village (18% mohair, 60% nylon, 22% acrylic, 138 yd [126 m]/50 g): #5557 white (GV), 2 (2, 2, 2, 3, 3) skeins. Lily Chin Signature Collection Times Square (21% cotton, 18% merino wool, 38% nylon, 21% acrylic, 2% metallic polyester, 115 yd [105 m]/50 g): #3393 white (TS), 3 (3, 3, 3, 4, 4) skeins.

Crochet hook: Size G/6 (4 mm). Adjust hook size if necessary to obtain the correct gauge.

Gauge

17 hdc and 11 hdc rows = 4" (10 cm) when worked through the FRONT lps of all sts, steam-blocked, and hung up.

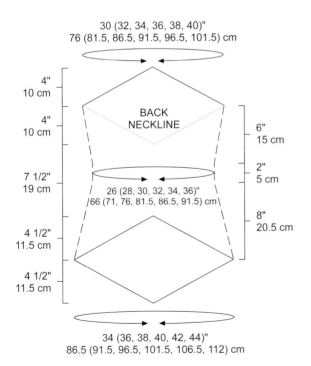

30 (32, 34, 36, 38, 40)"
76 (81.5, 86.5, 91.5, 96.5, 101.5) cm

4"
10 cm

4"
10 cm

BACK NECKLINE

6"
15 cm

7 1/2"
19 cm

26 (28, 30, 32, 34, 36)"
66 (71, 76, 81.5, 86.5, 91.5) cm

2"
5 cm

8"
20.5 cm

4 1/2"
11.5 cm

4 1/2"
11.5 cm

34 (36, 38, 40, 42, 44)"
86.5 (91.5, 96.5, 101.5, 106.5, 112) cm

Notes

- Body is worked in one piece in the round, beg and ending at center back. Ch 1s at beg of rows do not count as a st.
- Waist and bust shaping take place at the halter's sides, centered midway between the front and back chevrons. Note that the waist shaping decreases and the bust shaping increases do *not* stack one on top of another; rather, they shift toward the front, due to the biasing of the chevrons.
- Carry color not in use loosely at WS of work.

Special Stitches

Hdc inc: Working through front lps, work 2 hdc's into next st.

Hdc dec: Working through front lps, yo hook and pick up lp in next hdc, twice, yo hook and go through all 5 lps on hook.

Stripe Sequence

Work 2 rnds with GV, changing to TS at last st.
*Work 2 rnds with TS, changing to GV at last st.
Work 4 rnds with GV, changing to TS at last st.
Rep from * for Stripe Sequence.

Body

With GV, very loosely ch 172 (180, 188, 200, 208, 220).
Join with sl st to first ch to form circle, being careful not to twist.
Begin working Stripe Sequence, forming chevrons as follows:

Rnd 1 (RS): Ch 1 and turn, working into each ch around in hdc, hdc dec, *hdc in each of next 83 (87, 91, 97, 101, 107) ch*, [hdc inc] twice, rep from * to *, hdc dec, join with sl st to first st—172 (180, 188, 200, 208, 220) sts.

Rnd 2 (WS): Ch 1 and turn, working into front lps of each hdc, hdc dec, *hdc in each of next 83 (87, 91, 97, 101, 107) sts*, [hdc inc] twice, rep from * to *, hdc dec, join with sl st to first st—172 (180, 188, 200, 208, 220) sts.

Shape for Waist

Rnd 3: Ch 1 and turn, working into front lps of each hdc, hdc dec, *hdc in each of next 39 (41, 43, 46, 48, 51) hdc, hdc dec, hdc in next hdc, hdc dec, hdc in each of next 39 (41, 43, 46, 48, 51) hdc*, [hdc inc] twice, rep from * to *, hdc dec, join with sl st to first st—168 (176, 184, 196, 204, 216) sts.

Rnd 4: Ch 1 and turn, working into front lps of each hdc, hdc dec, *hdc in each of next 81 (85, 89, 95, 99, 105) sts*, [hdc inc] twice, rep from * to *, hdc dec, join with sl st to first st—168 (176, 184, 196, 204, 216) sts.

Rnd 5: Ch 1 and turn, working into front lps of each hdc, hdc dec, *hdc in each of next 38 (40, 42, 45, 47, 50) hdc, hdc dec, hdc in next hdc, hdc dec, hdc in each of next 38 (40, 42, 45, 47, 50) hdc*, [hdc inc] twice, rep from * to *, hdc dec, join with sl st to first st—164 (172, 180, 192, 200, 212) sts.

Rnd 6: Ch 1 and turn, working into front lps of each hdc, hdc dec, *hdc in each of next 79 (83, 87, 93, 97, 103) sts*, [hdc inc] twice, rep from * to *, hdc dec, join with sl st to first st—164 (172, 180, 192, 200, 212) sts.

Rnd 7: Ch 1 and turn, working into front lps of each hdc, hdc dec, *hdc in each of next 37 (39, 41, 44, 46, 49) hdc, hdc dec, hdc in next hdc, hdc dec, hdc in each of next 37 (39, 41, 44, 46, 49) hdc*, [hdc inc] twice, rep from * to *, hdc dec, join with sl st to first st—160 (168, 176, 188, 196, 208) sts.

Rnd 8: Ch 1 and turn, working into front lps of each hdc, hdc dec, *hdc in each of next 77 (81, 85, 91, 95, 101) sts*, [hdc inc] twice, rep from * to *, hdc dec, join with sl st to first st—160 (168, 176, 188, 196, 208) sts.

Rnd 9: Ch 1 and turn, working into front lps of each hdc, hdc dec, *hdc in each of next 36 (38, 40, 43, 45, 48) hdc, hdc dec, hdc in next hdc, hdc dec, hdc in each of next 36 (38, 40, 43, 45, 48) hdc*, [hdc inc] twice, rep from * to *, hdc dec, join with sl st to first st—156 (164, 172, 184, 192, 204) sts.

Rnd 10: Ch 1 and turn, working into front lps of each hdc, hdc dec, *hdc in each of next 75 (79, 83, 89, 93, 99) sts*, [hdc inc] twice, rep from * to *, hdc dec, join with sl st to first st—156 (164, 172, 184, 192, 204) sts.

Rnd 11: Ch 1 and turn, working into front lps of each hdc, hdc dec, *hdc in each of next 35 (37, 39, 42, 44, 47) hdc, hdc dec, hdc in next hdc, hdc dec, hdc in each of next 35 (37, 39, 42, 44, 47) hdc*, [hdc inc] twice, rep from * to *, hdc dec, join with sl st to first st—152 (160, 168, 180, 188, 200) sts.

Rnd 12: Ch 1 and turn, working into front lps of each hdc, hdc dec, *hdc in each of next 73 (77, 81, 87, 91, 97) sts*, [hdc inc] twice, rep from * to *, hdc dec, join with sl st to first st—152 (160, 168, 180, 188, 200) sts.

Rnd 13: Ch 1 and turn, working into front lps of each hdc, hdc dec, *hdc in each of next 34 (36, 38, 41, 43, 46) hdc, hdc dec, hdc in next hdc, hdc dec, hdc in each of next 34 (36, 38, 41, 43, 46) hdc*, [hdc inc] twice, rep from * to *, hdc dec, join with sl st to first st—148 (156, 164, 176, 184, 196) sts.

Rnd 14: Ch 1 and turn, working into front lps of each hdc, hdc dec, *hdc in each of next 71 (75, 79, 85, 89, 95) sts*, [hdc inc] twice, rep from * to *, hdc dec, join with sl st to first st—148 (156, 164, 176, 184, 196) sts.

Rnd 15: Ch 1 and turn, working into front lps of each hdc, hdc dec, *hdc in each of next 33 (35, 37, 40, 42, 45) hdc, hdc dec, hdc in next hdc, hdc dec, hdc in each of next 33 (35, 37, 40, 42, 45) hdc*, [hdc inc] twice, rep from * to *, hdc dec, join with sl st to first st—144 (152, 160, 172, 180, 192) sts.

Rnd 16: Ch 1 and turn, working into front lps of each hdc, hdc dec, *hdc in each of next 69 (73, 77, 83, 87, 93) sts*, [hdc inc] twice, rep from * to *, hdc dec, join with sl st to first st—144 (152, 160, 172, 180, 192) sts.

Rnd 17: Ch 1 and turn, working into front lps of each hdc, hdc dec, *hdc in each of next 32 (34, 36, 39, 41, 44) hdc, hdc dec, hdc in next hdc, hdc dec, hdc in each of next 32 (34, 36, 39, 41, 44) hdc*, [hdc inc] twice, rep from * to *, hdc dec, join with sl st to first st—140 (148, 156, 168, 176, 188) sts.

Rnd 18: Ch 1 and turn, working into front lps of each hdc, hdc dec, *hdc in each of next 67 (71, 75, 81, 85, 91) sts*, [hdc inc] twice, rep from * to *, hdc dec, join with sl st to first st—140 (148, 156, 168, 176, 188) sts.

Rnd 19: Ch 1 and turn, working into front lps of each hdc, hdc dec, *hdc in each of next 31 (33, 35, 38, 40, 43) hdc, hdc dec, hdc in next hdc, hdc dec, hdc in each of next 31 (33, 35, 38, 40, 43) hdc*, [hdc inc] twice, rep from * to *, hdc dec, join with sl st to first st—136 (144, 152, 164, 172, 184) sts.

Rnd 20: Ch 1 and turn, working into front lps of each hdc, hdc dec, *hdc in each of next 65 (69, 73, 79, 83, 89) sts*, [hdc inc] twice, rep from * to *, hdc dec, join with sl st to first st—136 (144, 152, 164, 172, 184) sts.

Rnds 21 and 22: Rep Rnd 20.

Shape for Bust

Rnd 23: Ch 1 and turn, working into front lps of each hdc, hdc dec, *hdc in each of next 31 (33, 35, 38, 40, 43) hdc, hdc inc, hdc in next hdc, hdc inc, hdc in each of next 31 (33, 35, 38, 40, 43) hdc*, [hdc inc] twice, rep from * to *, hdc dec, join with sl st to first st—140 (148, 156, 168, 176, 188) sts.

Rnds 24 and 25: Ch 1 and turn, working into front lps of each hdc, hdc dec, *hdc in each of next 67 (71, 75, 81, 85, 91) sts*, [hdc inc] twice, rep from * to *, hdc dec, join with sl st to first st—140 (148, 156, 168, 176, 188) sts.

Rnd 26: Ch 1 and turn, working into front lps of each hdc, hdc dec, *hdc in each of next 32 (34, 36, 39, 41, 44) hdc, hdc inc, hdc in next hdc, hdc inc, hdc in each of next 32 (34, 36, 39, 41, 44) hdc*, [hdc inc] twice, rep from * to *, hdc dec, join with sl st to first st—144 (152, 160, 172, 180, 192) sts.

Rnds 27 and 28: Ch 1 and turn, working into front lps of each hdc, hdc dec, *hdc in each of next 69 (73, 77, 83, 87, 93) sts*, [hdc inc] twice, rep from * to *, hdc dec, join with sl st to first st—144 (152, 160, 172, 180, 192) sts.

Rnd 29: Ch 1 and turn, working into front lps of each hdc, hdc dec, *hdc in each of next 33 (35, 37, 40, 42, 45) hdc, hdc inc, hdc in next hdc, hdc inc, hdc in each of next 33 (35, 37, 40, 42, 45) hdc*, [hdc inc] twice, rep from * to *, hdc dec, join with sl st to first st—148 (156, 164, 176, 184, 196) sts.

Rnds 30 and 31: Ch 1 and turn, working into front lps of each hdc, hdc dec, *hdc in each of next 71 (75, 79, 85, 89, 95) sts*, [hdc inc] twice, rep from * to *, hdc dec, join with sl st to first st—148 (156, 164, 176, 184, 196) sts.

Rnd 32: Ch 1 and turn, working into front lps of each hdc, hdc dec, *hdc in each of next 34 (36, 38, 41, 43, 46) hdc, hdc inc, hdc in next hdc, hdc inc, hdc in each of next 34 (36, 38, 41, 43, 46) hdc*, [hdc inc] twice, rep from * to *, hdc dec, join with sl st to first st—152 (160, 168, 180, 188, 200) sts.

Rnds 33–36: Ch 1 and turn, working into front lps of each hdc, hdc dec, *hdc in each of next 73 (77, 81, 87, 91, 97) sts*, [hdc inc] twice, rep from * to *, hdc dec, join with sl st to first st—152 (160, 168, 180, 188, 200) sts.

Rnd 37: Ch 1 and turn, sc through BOTH lps of each st around, join with sl st to first sc, fasten and end off.

Finishing

Block piece to measurements.

Straps

First Strap

With WS facing, join to one of top sc at center front neck, ch 1, sc in same sc.

All subsequent rows: Ch 1 and turn, sc in sc. Work until strap measures 18" (45.5 cm) or until desired length. Fasten and end off, leaving 6" (15 cm) tail.

Second Strap

With WS facing, join to other of top sc at center front neck. Work as for first strap.

Using tail, sew straps to back where bra straps might begin.

Gloves

Finished Size

Women's glove size 5 (6, 7, 8). Sample is worked in size 6.

Materials

Yarn: Lily Chin Signature Collection Greenwich Village (18% mohair, 60% nylon, 22% acrylic, 138 yd [126 m]/50 g): #5557 white (GV), 2 (2, 2, 2) skeins. Lily Chin Signature Collection Times Square (21% cotton, 18% merino wool, 38% nylon, 21% acrylic, 2% metallic polyester, 115 yd [105 m]/50 g): #3393 white (TS), 1 (1, 2, 2) skeins.

Crochet hook: Size G/6 (4 mm). Adjust hook size if necessary to obtain the correct gauge.

Gauge

18 sc and 15 sc rows = 4" (10 cm) when worked through the FRONT lps of all sts, steam-blocked, and hung up.

Notes

- Body is worked in one piece in the round, beg and ending at center back of hand. Inc in width of piece is primarily achieved by changing frequency of inc/dec rnd and thus angle of chevron.
- Carry color not in use loosely at WS of work.

Special Stitches

Sc inc: Working through front lps, work 2 sc into one st.
Sc dec: Working through front lps, twice, yo hook and go through all 3 lps on hook.

Stripe Sequence

Work 2 rnds with GV, changing to TS at last st.
*Work 2 rnds with TS, changing to GV at last st.
Work 4 rnds with GV, changing to TS at last st.
Rep from * for Stripe Sequence.

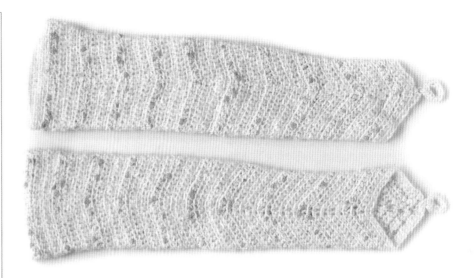

Finger Ring

With GV, very loosely ch enough to go around middle finger, join with sl st to beg of ch to form circle. Ch 1, sc in each sc around, join with sl st to first sc. Do not cut yarn.

Body

Very loosely ch 36 (40, 44, 48). Join with sl st to first ch to form circle, being careful not to twist.

Begin working Stripe Sequence, forming chevrons as follows:

Rnd 1 (RS): Ch 1, sc dec, sc in each of next 15 (17, 19, 21) ch, [sc inc] twice, sc in each of next 15 (17, 19, 21) ch, sc dec, join with sl st to first st—36 (40, 44, 48) sts.

Rnd 2 (inc/dec rnd): Ch 1 and turn. Working into front lps of each sc, sc dec, *sc in each of next 15 (17, 19, 21) sc*, [sc inc] twice, rep from * to *, sc dec, join with sl st to first st—36 (40, 44, 48) sts.

Rnds 3–12: Rep Rnd 2.

Rnd 13 (non-inc/dec rnd): Ch 1 and turn, sc into front

lps of each sc around, join with sl st to first st—36 (40, 44, 48) sts.

Rnd 14: Rep Rnd 2.

Rnds 15–22: Rep Rnds 13 and 14, working inc/dec rnd only every other rnd.

Rnds 23 and 24: Rep Rnd 13.

Rnd 25: Rep Rnd 2.

Rnds 26–34: Rep Rnds 23–25, working inc/dec rnd only every 3rd rnd.

Rnds 35–37: Rep Rnd 13.

Rnd 38: Rep Rnd 2.

Rnds 39–46: Rep Rnds 35–38, working inc/dec rnd only every 4th rnd.

Rnds 47–51: Rep Rnd 13.

Rnd 52: Rep Rnd 2.

Rnd 53: Ch 1 and turn. Working into front lps of each sc, sc in each of first 8 (9, 10, 11) sc, *sc inc, sc in next sc, sc inc*, sc in each of next 14 (16, 18, 20) sc, rep from * to *, sc in each of last 8 (9, 10, 11) sc, join with sl st to first st—40 (44, 48, 52) sts.

Rnds 54–60: Rep Rnd 13.

Fasten and end off.

Finishing

Block piece to measurements.

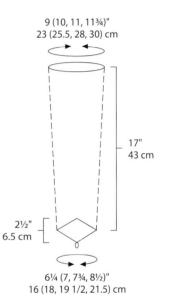

9 (10, 11, 11¾)"
23 (25.5, 28, 30) cm

17"
43 cm

2½"
6.5 cm

6¼ (7, 7¾, 8½)"
16 (18, 19 1/2, 21.5) cm

Abbreviations

beg	begin(s); beginning	rep	repeat; repeating
bet	between	rev sc	reverse single crochet
CC	contrasting color	rnd(s)	round(s)
ch	chain	RS	right side
cm	centimeter(s)	sc	single crochet
cont	continue(s); continuing	sk	skip
dc	double crochet	sl	slip
dec(s)('d)	decrease(s); decreasing; decreased	sl st	slip(ped) stitch
est	established	sp(s)	space(es)
foll	follows; following	st(s)	stitch(es)
g	gram(s)	tog	together
hdc	half double crochet	tr	treble crochet
inc(s)('d)	increase(s); increasing; increased	WS	wrong side
lp(s)	loops(s)	yd	yard
m	marker	yo	yarn over
MC	main color	*	repeat starting point
mm	millimeter(s)	**	repeat all instructions between asterisks
patt(s)	pattern(s)	()	alternate measurements and/or instructions
pm	place marker	[]	work bracketed instructions a specified number of times
rem	remain(s); remaining		

Sources for Further Reading

Amaden-Crawford, Connie. *The Art of Fashion Draping* (2nd Ed.). New York: Fairchild Books & Visuals, 1995.

Brown, Nancy. *The Crocheter's Companion*. Loveland, Colorado: Interweave Press, 2002.

Jaffe, Hilde and Nurie Relis. *Draping for Fashion Design* (4th Ed.). Upper Saddle River, NJ: Prentice-Hall Career & Technology, 2004.

Newton, Deborah. *Designing Knitwear*. Newtown, Connecticut: The Taunton Press, 1998.

Rohr Mayer. *Draping: Women's and Misses' Garment Design*. Montclair, NJ: Rohr Publishing Co., 1987.

Suppliers

Materials featured in this book have been supplied by:

Berroco Inc., PO Box 367, 14 Elmdale Rd., Uxbridge, MA 01569; (508) 278-2527; www.berroco.com.

Brown Sheep Company, 100662 County Rd. 16, Mitchell, NE 69357; (800) 826-9136; www.brownsheep.com.

Cascade Yarns, 1224 Andover Park E., Tukwila, WA 98188; (206) 574-0440; www.cascadeyarns.com.

Earth Bead Gallery, 2634 N. 48th St., Lincoln, NE 68504; (402) 467-2244; earthbead@aol.com; www.earthbeadgallery.com.

Karabella Yarns, 1201 Broadway, New York, NY 10001; (212) 684-2665; (800) 550-0898; info@karabellayarns.com; www.karabellayarns.com.

Lily Chin Signature Collection, 5333 Casgrain Ave., Ste 1204, Montreal, Qc, Canada H2T 1X3; (514) 276-1204; (877) 244-1204; info@lilychinsignaturecollection.com; www.lilychinsignaturecollection.com.

Louet Sales, 808 Commerce Park Dr., Ogdensburg, NY 13669; (613) 925-4502; info@louet.com; www.louet.com.

Mission Falls, 5333 Casgrain Ave., Ste. 1204, Montreal, QC, Canada, H2T 1X3; (514) 276-1204; (877) 244-1204; info@missionfalls.com; www.missionfalls.com.

Plymouth Yarn Company Inc., PO Box 28, Bristol, PA 19007; (215) 788-0459; pyc@plymouthyarn.com; www.plymouthyarn.com.

Sulyn Industries Inc., 11927 W. Sample Rd., Coral Springs, FL 33065; (954) 755-2311; www.sulyn.com.

Trendsetter Yarns, 16745 Saticoy St., Ste. 101, Van Nuys, CA 91406; (818) 780-5497; (800) 446-2425; info@trendsetteryarns.com; www.trendsetteryarns.com.

Westminster Fibers Inc., 18 Celina Ave., Ste. 17, Nashua, NH 03063; (800) 445-9276; linda.pratt@ westminsterfibers.com; www.westminsterfibers.com.

To generate any gauge of graph paper or grid paper: www.tata-tatao.to/knit/matrix/e-index.html.

For Print-A-Grid software: Knitting Software Inc., 4104 Landing Ln., Moon Township, PA 15108; (412) 264-1953; www.knittingsoftware.com.

For Garment Designer and Stitch Painter software: Cochenille Design Studio, PO Box 235604, Encinitas, CA 92023-5604; (858) 259-1698; (760) 393-2344; info@cochenille.com; www.cochenille.com.

For a custom dress form (made out of duct tape): www.leanna.com/DuctTapeDouble.

Grid paper and gridded flip charts can be pruchased at any large office supply store, such as Office Depot, Office Max, or Staples.

Index